The Vegetable Sushi Cookbook

Recipes for the sushi on this page can be found on pages 99 and 100.

The Vegetable Sushi Cookbook

Izumi Shoji

PHOTOGRAPHS BY **Noriko Yamaguchi**

TRANSLATED BY **Deborah Iwabuchi**

KODANSHA USA

The author would like to thank Radish Boya for their fresh produce,
Kinto Co., Ltd., Space Takamori, Chidori and noda horo co., ltd. for
the use of their dinnerware, and Kamawanu Co., Ltd. for their *tenugui.*

Published by Kodansha USA, Inc.
451 Park Avenue South
New York, NY 10016

Distributed in the United Kingdom and continental Europe
by Kodansha Europe Ltd.

Originally published in Japanese in 2010 by Kodansha International,
in a slightly different form, under the title izumimirun no Yasaino Osushi
English publication rights arranged with Kodansha Ltd.

ISBN 978-1-56836-570-1
First edition, 2016
21 20 19 18 17 16   10 9 8 7 6 5 4 3 2 1
Library of Congress Cataloging-in-Publication Data

Names: Shōji, Izumi, 1965- | Yamaguchi, Noriko (Photographer)
Title: The vegetable sushi cookbook / Izumi Shoji ; photographs by
Noriko
   Yamaguchi ; translated by Deborah Iwabuchi.
Other titles: Izumimirun no yasai no osushi. English
Description: New York, NY : Kodansha USA, 2016. | Includes index.
Identifiers: LCCN 2015038108 | ISBN 9781568365701
Subjects: LCSH: Sushi. | Cooking, Japanese. | Cooking (Rice) | Cooking
   (Vegetables) | LCGFT: Cookbooks.
Classification: LCC TX724.5.J3 S54813 2016 | DDC 641.5952--dc23
LC record available at http://lccn.loc.gov/2015038108

www.kodanshausa.com

Contents

Foreword

I am not a chef at a famous restaurant. I am not a teacher at a culinary academy. I am a Japanese housewife who fell in love with vegetables, and for some reason, it's a relationship that has completely changed my life.

When I gave birth to my daughter (who's now a healthy high schooler), I had a lot of physical problems which prompted me to begin studying what I ate and wanting to learn how I could become healthier. What I discovered about food led me on the path to becoming, about ten years ago, a full-time vegetarian.

Vegetables, it seems, were a perfect match for me, and it was not long before all my health problems were solved. I did, however, have another problem. I love to eat. I've always loved to eat, and I like eating lots of food, and I like lots of variety in what I eat. I also love to cook. I searched the bookstores to find something that would match my attitude, but at the time, there were very few books around. Maybe it was because Japanese cuisine has always been focused on vegetables, so no one thought a book on vegetarian cooking would have a market. There were books on macrobiotics, but it all seemed so complex to me. I was looking for something fun, something simple, something that would offer recipes as tasty as any other cuisine.

But I came up empty. It got me thinking about writing a book, but I soon realized that it was impossible for a complete amateur to get a publishing contract. A blog, though, was a whole different story.

In February 2007, I launched my blog featuring the kinds of vegetarian recipes that I had been looking for: unique recipes for vegetarian hamburgers, vegetarian gyoza, omelets, and more. They could all be made in minutes, which seemed to be a huge selling point: readership of my blog soared, interest grew—and barely a year later, I had my first cookbook released by a major publisher. Many more were to come; I now have over fifty books on Japanese bookstore shelves.

When talk of doing a book in English surfaced, my thoughts went wild. Do I introduce traditional dishes, sticking to traditional tastes? Materials? Methods? But the more I thought about it, the more I found reasons to do one thing most of all: a book of vegetable sushi.

First of all, sushi is a celebration of Japanese food culture. Not only does it ultimately depend on the basic Japanese idea about serving food—a desire to bring out the true taste of seasonal, fresh ingredients—but for Japanese people, the dish usually appears on special occasions—birthdays, anniversaries, and other parties, and special festivals like Girls' Day. There's a festive air about sushi, and it's unique, despite its popularity.

It's also very easy to make, which is extremely important to me as a busy housewife. Dishes like tempura may be popular, but the technique required can be quite difficult. With sushi, all you really need is rice, some vinegar, and some of your favorite ingredients.

And the price is right, especially compared to such Japanese dishes as sukiyaki or shabu shabu. It is surprising to find out how far vegetables and rice can go in feeding a lot of people, whether it's a big family or a large party.

Normally, sushi would mean fresh seafood and vegetables, but the recipes here call only for vegetables. (This should be a relief to anyone who has tried to slice fresh fish into truly attractive sushi material.) I've included traditional Japanese vegetables, which are becoming increasingly available around the world, and there are photos and explanations in the book so that you can track them down. I suggest that if you can't find them in local markets, visit an Asian market or—as is becoming more and more popular—look on the Internet. (I find it fascinating that spicy *yuzukosho*, for example, can be ordered online.)

I do offer alternatives, in case you have trouble finding some of the foods. I've tried to mix up the styles—nigiri-zushi, maki-zushi, maze-zushi, and more—and traditional Japanese-style cooking methods, including simmering, grilling, steaming, and frying, so that you'll find plenty of variety in taste, aroma, and color.

I also hope that this book inspires you to experiment, using fresh local ingredients in new ways. Sushi is a perfect cuisine because it can be made anywhere, using almost any kind of ingredient, as long as it's fresh and tasty.

If you ever thought good food means a lot of work, I hope I can change your mind. Have fun, cook less, eat well, and enjoy every last bite of delicious vegetable sushi.*

Izumi Shoji
Tokyo 2011

*By the way, you'll see the words "sushi" and "zushi" used throughout this book. In Japanese, when the word "sushi" is used in combination with another word, it is pronounced "zushi."

Deep-fried King Oyster Mushroom Nigiri-zushi
Deep-fried Japanese Leek Maki-zushi

recipes on page 100

Burdock Root Steamed with Soy Sauce Maki-zushi
Japanese Leek Steamed with Miso Nigiri-zushi

recipes on page 101

How to Make the Perfect Sushi Rice

When it comes to sushi, it all starts with the rice. No matter how delectable your toppings are, they won't taste their best unless the sushi rice is perfect. Each grain should be firm and shiny, and the rice should offer both the sweet aroma of the grain and the piquancy of sushi. When popped in your mouth, it should be neither too sweet nor too sour—the ideal taste is mellow. Since all of these recipes are quite easy to make, you'll find that when your rice is ready, you'll soon be dining on vegetable sushi.

Making the perfect sushi rice is not difficult. Wash the dry rice and let it drain in a colander for about 30 minutes before putting it in a rice cooker, clay pot, or other cooking pot. If you use a rice cooker, you will most likely find lines marked on the inside of the pot to measure water for sushi rice. When using a clay pot or other cooking vessel, use 180 ml of water for 1 cup of dry rice, 360 ml for 2 cups, and 540 ml for 3 cups. This is about 10 percent less water than usual for rice, because extra liquid in the form of vinegar will be added after it is cooked.

Most rice cookers only require the press of a button to start. To cook rice in a clay pot on the stovetop, combine the water and rice in the pot over moderate heat. Bring to a boil (this takes about 5 minutes), then lower the heat so that it doesn't boil over; cook for 10 minutes. Resist the temptation to open the lid! After 10 minutes, turn the heat up to high for just 10 seconds, then remove from heat. Let the rice steam for another 15 minutes before adding vinegar and other ingredients. If rice is not allowed to steam enough in the last step, it will be soft and overly sticky. You can also make rice in a metal pot, but be sure the bottom and sides are thick enough to make the rice fluffy.

ADDING THE VINEGAR MIXTURE

Rice vinegar without added seasoning should be used for making sushi rice unless otherwise indicated. Quantities of vinegar and sugar for varying amounts of rice are provided in the chart below. Note that vegetable sushi tastes better when the rice is slightly sweeter compared to sushi topped with fish. "Basic sushi rice" in the chart is fine for any kind of vegetable sushi you plan to make.

One drawback of slightly sweeter sushi rice is that it tends to tire the palate. If this happens, try the "mild-flavored sushi rice," which is not as sweet. Some of the recipes in this book use rice seasoned with lemon juice, grapefruit juice, or balsamic vinegar, so there are different varieties to try with the different toppings. Try them all and discover which combinations you like best.

1   When the rice is fully steamed, turn it out into a wooden sushi tub or other large bowl while still hot. Gently stir in the vinegar mixture with a rice paddle. Break apart any large masses of rice.

2   Spread the rice over the bottom of the tub and continue to cut in the vinegar mixture with the rice paddle, making sure it is thoroughly mixed in.

3   Next, have an assistant fan the rice to cool it as you gently scoop the rice up from the bottom and distribute the seasoning. The breeze helps the vinegar mixture blend in as the rice cools, and gives the rice a shiny appearance.

4   Wet a towel, thoroughly wring out the excess water, and lay it over the rice. When the rice cools to room temperature it is ready to eat. If sushi rice is too hot, it will

ruin the toppings. If it's too cool, it will be difficult to mix in ingredients (as for maze-zushi), or to spread onto nori for maki-zushi. The ideal temperature for sushi rice is room temperature.

INGREDIENT CHART FOR VINEGARED SUSHI RICE

One 180 cc rice-cooker cup (just over ¾ of a US cup, or 6 oz / 170 g) of dry rice yields 1¾ cups (330 g) of cooked rice.

Basic sushi rice

1¾ cups (330 g) cooked rice	1⅔ Tbsp rice vinegar	1 Tbsp sugar	½ tsp salt
3½ cups (660 g) cooked rice	3 Tbsp rice vinegar	2 Tbsp sugar	1 tsp salt
5¼ cups (990 g) cooked rice	5 Tbsp rice vinegar	3 Tbsp sugar	1½ tsp salt

Mild sushi rice

1¾ cups (330 g) cooked rice	1½ Tbsp rice vinegar	½ Tbsp sugar	½ tsp salt
3½ cups (660 g) cooked rice	3 Tbsp rice vinegar	1 Tbsp sugar	1 tsp salt
5¼ cups (990 g) cooked rice	5 Tbsp rice vinegar	1½ Tbsp sugar	1½ tsp salt

Lemon sushi rice

1¾ cups (330 g) cooked rice	1⅔ Tbsp lemon juice	½ Tbsp sugar	½ tsp salt

Grapefruit sushi rice

1¾ cups (330 g) cooked rice	1⅓ Tbsp grapefruit juice	2 scant tsp rice vinegar	½ Tbsp sugar	½ tsp salt

Umeboshi plum sushi rice

1¾ cups (330 g) cooked rice	2 large umeboshi plums (remove the pits and break up the pulp with the back edge of the knife before mixing with the rice)

Balsamic vinegar rice

1¾ cups (330 g) cooked rice	1½ Tbsp balsamic vinegar	1 tsp sugar	½ tsp salt

HOW TO MAKE SHIITAKE AND KONBU DASHI STOCK

Dashi stock is a fundamental element of Japanese food. You may find it convenient to make a large batch and keep in on hand rather than make it fresh every time you need it. Basic dashi is traditionally made with konbu and dried bonito shavings, but I recommend using dashi made only with vegetables for vegetarian sushi so that the flavor doesn't overwhelm the taste of the other ingredients.

The shiitake and konbu dashi here is good for soups, simmering, and other recipes, and it's extremely simple to make. You can freeze it in an ice-cube tray and store the cubes in a sealed plastic bag to make small amounts handy.

Ingredients for 1 quart (1 liter) of dashi stock:

1 quart (1 liter) water
2 x 4 in (5 x 10 cm) piece of dashi konbu, broken into small pieces
3–4 dried shiitake mushrooms

Combine the water, konbu, and shiitake in a covered glass or plastic pitcher and refrigerate for a few hours or overnight. Remove the konbu and shiitake, and the dashi is ready for use. (Do not leave the konbu in for more than 12 hours or it will make the dashi slimy.)

Vegetable Sushi Ingredients

Here are most of the vegetables and condiments that appear in the recipes. Many of them were once only available in Japan, but with the rise in interest in Japanese and other Asian cuisines, they are now available in various forms from markets or on the Internet. Feel free, of course, to try your own substitutions and alternatives; there's nothing like discovering a new dish that came from a burst of inspiration.

Burdock Root (*gobo*): This long, fibrous root has an earthy sweetness that is reminiscent of artichokes (and in fact, both are members of the thistle family). Burdock root should be soaked in cold water or vinegar water after cutting to prevent browning and to remove some of the harsh-tasting tannins, and should be cooked well. Salsify, though not as mellow in flavor, may be a reasonable substitute if burdock is not available.

Cooking saké: Saké, also called rice wine, is brewed (like beer) rather than being distilled or fermented (like vodka or wine). While saké dedicated for cooking is available (much as "cooking wine" is in the West), using an inexpensive brew suitable for drinking will give better results.

Daikon Radish: A long, thick root vegetable that is a staple of Asian cuisine. This relative of the radish is quite mild and can be eaten raw or cooked. The part furthest from the stem has a sharper flavor; *daikon* radish is also sweeter in winter.

Dashi Konbu: The high glutamic acid content of *konbu*, a sea vegetable of the genus *Laminaria*, lends a rich flavor to any dish. Like other dried sea vegetables, konbu should be kept in an airtight container in a cool, dark place. Do not wash in water before using, as the white powder on the surface is an important flavoring component—just wipe away any foreign particles with a damp towel.

Deep-fried tofu (*abura-age*): Abura-age is made from tofu that is thinly sliced and deep-fried twice. The process forms a kind of pouch with a chewy consistency that absorbs flavoring and liquid beautifully. Abura-age is usually blanched and rinsed before using to get rid of the excess oil. Use abura-age soon after purchasing; it can also be frozen for up to 6 months.

Enoki Mushrooms: The long, thin stems and crisp texture of *enoki* mushrooms (also called snow mushrooms or winter mushrooms) make them seem as much like a vegetable as a fungus. They grow in clusters, and the cultivated mushrooms available in markets are grown specifically to be long-stemmed and creamy white. They should be washed gently and the spongy base trimmed off before eating fresh or cooking. Check them for freshness before buying (they should not be slimy) and use them within a few days.

Freeze-dried Tofu (*koya-dofu*): Freeze-dried tofu is usually sold in boxes or cellophane-wrapped squares. To reconstitute, soak in warm water for about 5 minutes, then drain off the water and squeeze the tofu gently before cutting as needed. Store it in a cool dry place. Be aware that it does not keep well and will develop an unpleasant flavor over time, so use soon after purchasing.

Goya: This member of the gourd family, known as bitter melon, is widely used in southern Asian cuisine. Originally from India, goya has long been a feature of Okinawan cuisine, and is now eaten throughout mainland Japan. It is reputed to have significant health benefits—Okinawans credit it with helping them cope with the oppressive heat of summer, and even with giving them one of the world's highest life expectancies. True to its name, goya is very bitter, and many children have trouble eating it, but when properly cooked and combined with complementary flavors it is quite palatable to adults. Blanching or salting and rinsing goya after slicing will remove some of the bitter flavor. Scrape out the seeds and pith from inside the gourd before using.

Green Spring Onion (*banno-negi*): This thin, mild variety of spring onion is mainly eaten raw (the name translates to "all-purpose onion"). Green onions or scallions make an acceptable, if somewhat sharper, substitute.

Hijiki: One of the first sea vegetables to be used widely in the West, *hijiki* has a rich flavor reminiscent of the sea. Like all sea vegetables, it is high in fiber and essential minerals, particularly calcium. It is generally sold dried; in this form it looks a bit like loose-leaf black tea. Keep it in an airtight container stored in a cool, dark place; use a desiccant pack in the container if you live in a humid area.

Japanese cucumber: These are slenderer than their European counterparts, with thinner skin and tiny seeds. If they are unavailable, use peeled and seeded Western cucumbers.

Japanese eggplant: Long, slender Japanese eggplants tend to have thinner skin and a more delicate flavor than the larger fruits typically found in the West. Western eggplants can be used, but may need a longer cooking time and will become more watery when cooked.

Japanese Leek (*naganegi*): A thick spring onion with a long white stem section and tuberous green spears. Generally only the mild white flesh is used. In recipes that call for cooking, young leeks are an acceptable substitute; if raw, the white part of scallions or green onions can be used in its place.

Karashi Hot Mustard: Unlike common yellow mustard in the West, which is characterized by its vinegary tang, *karashi* is simply powdered mustard seed and water. It is available in tubes in Asian markets, or you can make your own by mixing equal parts water and dry English mustard. Add a bit of oil and let it rest, covered, for about 10 minutes to develop its full flavor.

King Oyster Mushrooms (*eringi*): These fat-stemmed mushrooms are also known as king trumpet mushrooms. While rather bland raw, cooked eringi have a rich mushroom aroma and meaty texture. They will keep for up to 2 weeks if stored in a loosely closed paper bag in the refrigerator.

Kiriboshi Daikon: Traditionally, daikon radish was cut into strips and sun-dried in winter to make *kiriboshi* (cut-and-dried) *daikon*. It has a rather sweet flavor and chewy texture, and absorbs seasonings very well. Kiriboshi daikon has a strong odor before it is washed and soaked, but this quickly disappears. Briefly wash the kiriboshi daikon before soaking, and reserve the soaking water for cooking.

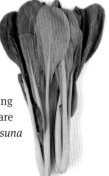

Komatsuna: A mild leafy green in the brassica family, sometimes called Japanese mustard spinach. Spinach, young swiss chard, or baby bok choy are acceptable substitutes if *komatsuna* is unavailable.

Lotus Root (*renkon*): The rhizome of the lotus plant is a starchy tuber with a crisp texture and delicate flavor. Lotus roots should be peeled before use. Slicing the root will reveal its lacy interior—the holes inside should be washed well, as they can be muddy. Soak cut lotus root in vinegar water to prevent browning.

Maitake Mushrooms: Known in English as "hen-of-the-woods," this mushroom—a type of bracket fungus—comprises a cluster of delicate cream-colored fans with brown tips. *Maitake* are esteemed for their earthy savor when cooked, and are widely held to have cancer-inhibiting properties. They need no washing and should be torn, rather than cut, into bite-sized pieces before cooking. Maitake will keep for about a week if stored in a loosely closed paper bag in the refrigerator.

Mirin: True mirin is a sweet, alcohol-based seasoning brewed naturally from rice. Too often, however, it is a syrupy mixture of synthetic alcohol and added sweetener. Try to find naturally brewed mirin. To replace 1 tablespoon of mirin, use 1 tablespoon of saké plus 2 teaspoons sugar.

Nori: Square sheets of purplish *nori*—made from laver that is pounded smooth and dried on screens like handmade paper—turn bright green when roasted and have a delightful crunch. Nori is usually sold in roasted form. It quickly turns limp and stale, and should be kept in an airtight tin with a desiccant pack to minimize moisture. It is best to buy nori in small quantities, as it does not keep as long as other dried sea vegetables. Limp nori can restored to crispness by toasting in a very low oven for 10 minutes.

Red miso: Red miso typically contains barley or other grains, but has a greater proportion of soybeans than white miso, and is fermented for at least a year. It is stronger and saltier than white miso.

Rice vinegar: Brewed with the ever-useful *koji* (*A. oryzae*) bacillus, rice vinegar has a more mellow, rounded flavor than wine or white vinegar. Be sure to use rice vinegar that is *not* pre-seasoned. Substituting diluted white or cider vinegar is possible, but it is not recommended.

Shichimi Pepper: A popular spice blend in Japan, *shichimi* has dried red chili pepper as its main ingredient. The heat is rounded out by the other ingredients, which typically include roasted citrus peel, sesame or poppy seeds, and ground prickly ash berries (*sansho*). The name means "seven-flavor chili," but the proportions of the seasonings vary with the manufacturer.

Shiitake Mushrooms: These mushrooms are native to Asia, but are now widely cultivated throughout the northern hemisphere. They are valued for their superb flavor and meaty texture. They grow on fallen trees, and after harvesting are sold either fresh or dried. They will keep for about 10 days if stored in a loosely closed paper bag in the refrigerator.

Shimeji Mushrooms: Known as beech or clamshell mushrooms in English, these small brown or tan mushrooms grow in clusters on trees, and are in the same family as oyster mushrooms. They are native to Japan, but widely cultivated. Water will damage their flavor,

so they should be brushed off, or washed only very sparingly, before using. They will keep for about 10 days if stored in a loosely closed paper bag in the refrigerator.

Shiso: Best known as perilla in the West, this broad-leafed herb is also called beefsteak plant or Japanese basil. It comes in both green and red varieties; the green is most common. The quality of its flavor is not unlike that of basil or mint, but its herbal tang is unique. These or other herbs may be used in place of *shiso*, but the character of the dish will change completely.

Sushi rice: Different types of rice contain different proportions of the starches amylase and amylopectin; for example, short-grain rice is moist and sticky, while long-grain rice grains stay drier and separate when they are cooked. Sushi rice has a very short grain and a higher proportion of amylopectin starch than regular short-grain rice, making it very sticky. Unfortunately, other kinds of rice simply don't work well for sushi.

Tororo Yam (*nagaimo*): Often called "Chinese yam" in English, tororo yam is uniformly cylindrical, often stored in sawdust and sold in pre-cut lengths, with off-white skin that looks like it has goose pimples. Peel and rinse nagaimo under cold water before cutting. It can be eaten raw (it has a crisp, succulent crunch similar to jicama) and is also often ground or grated to make a glutinous paste. Care should be taken when handling or eating raw yam, as it may irritate the skin.

Umeboshi Plums: These salt-pickled fruits (actually a variety of apricot) have a unique piquant sourness. Many find the flavor overwhelming at first, but it is not hard to become accustomed to it. *Umeboshi* are reputed to have many health benefits such as tonifying and alkalinizing the blood.

White Turnip (*kabu*): The Japanese turnip is far smaller and milder than European or American turnips. They can be eaten raw, as the flesh is tender and slightly sweet, but are more often simmered, roasted, or pickled. The slightly bitter greens may be eaten as well. There really are no good substitutes for *kabu*.

Wakame: This tender, mild-flavored kelp has long, ribbon-like fronds that are deep green in color. Dried *wakame* should be soaked for 10 to 20 minutes before using; if uncut wakame is used, cut out the central vein of the leaf after soaking. Note that soaked dried wakame will expand to nearly 8 times its original volume.

Yuzukosho: This unique condiment is a coarsely ground mix of salt, *yuzu* (citron) peel, and chili peppers. Use it sparingly at first, but be warned that many who discover *yuzukosho* find themselves adding it to everything! Available at Asian markets or on the Internet.

Wasabi: This relative of horseradish grows only in clear, cold mountain streams. Though the fresh-ground root is incomparable for its sweet pungency, wasabi can also be bought in tubes or in powdered form. To reconstitute, place about 2 teaspoons in a small cup and add ice-cold water a little at a time, using a chopstick to stir rapidly, until it becomes a soft paste. Invert the cup over a saucer to prevent the flavor from evaporating.

White miso: Miso is a salty paste made by fermenting soybeans and grains (usually rice and/or barley) with *koji*, or *A. oryzae* spores, a fungus also used for making saké, mirin, and rice vinegar, among other foods. White miso has a high proportion of rice and a short fermentation period, and is milder and sweeter than red miso.

Mizuna: This is a bright green, spikey-leafed member of the mustard family. I haven't included it in any of the menus, but if you can find it at a local market, I suggest using it as a substitute for spinach, for example. The leaves can be eaten raw or cooked, and have a slightly peppery flavor.

Nigiri-zushi and Gunkan-maki

Many people believe that "real" sushi is only available at a sushi shop. But this really isn't so. You can make real sushi at home simply by making sushi rice, forming it into bite-sized pieces, and topping the result with your favorite ingredients. This is what we call *nigiri-zushi*. If you wrap a strip of nori around the edge of the piece of rice and add a topping, the result is *gunkan-maki*.

Making sushi with vegetables is even easier than making it with fish. Whether you select specific vegetables for party hors d'oeuvres or just use what is on hand for an everyday meal, making nigiri-zushi with vegetables is simply a matter of following a very few basic steps. Like good vegetables themselves, the results will be both colorful and rich with a variety of flavors.

Recipes for the sushi on this page can be found on pages 24 and 25.

How To Make Nigiri-zushi

1   Rice will stick to
dry hands, making it
difficult to shape, so
be sure your hands are
damp when forming
nigiri-zushi or otherwise
handling sushi rice. It's

best to prepare a 10-to-1 mixture of water and vinegar, and
use just enough to moisten your hands. If your hands are
too wet, the rice will become soggy.

2   Put about ¾ oz
(20 g, or about 1½ table-
spoons) of sushi rice in
your left hand. You don't
have to weigh each
piece. This should be
enough to make a bite-
sized piece of nigiri-
zushi.

3   Form a longish oval
of rice about ½ in tall,
1 in wide, and 2 in long
(2 x 3 x 5 cm) by cup-
ping the rice in your
left hand and shaping
it lightly with your right

index and middle fingers. Don't press it too hard—you
want the rice to be light and fluffy when you eat it. But if
you use too little pressure, the rice will fall apart before it
can be eaten.

4   Depending on the
topping, you might
want to add wasabi
at this stage. You can
either put a dab on the
shaped rice or spread it
thinly on the back of the
topping.

5   Arrange the topping
on the formed nigiri and
lightly press it down on
the rice. Your nigiri-zushi
is ready to eat!

How To Make Gunkan-maki

1   Take about ¾ oz
(20 g) of sushi rice and
form it into a nigiri
shape as described to
the left.

2   Wrap a 7 x 1 in (18
x 3.5 cm) strip of nori
around the rice to encir-
cle it. The nori should
be taller than the height
of the rice so that it will
hold the sushi topping
in place.

3   If the ends of the
nori strip overlap by
more than ½ in (1 cm),
trim off the excess. Press
a single grain of rice
between the ends of the
nori strip to glue them
together.

4   Place the topping
on the rice. If the top-
ping is soft or fluid, it is
best to use a spoon.

Shiitake Mushroom and Mustard Nigiri-zushi

The spice and tang of mustard go very well with the sushi rice. There's already plenty of flavor in these, so they don't need to be dipped in soy sauce. (They go very well with wine, by the way.)

Ingredients for 4 pieces:

3 medium fresh shiitake mushrooms (1¾ oz / 50 g total)
1 tsp whole-grain mustard
1 Tbsp saké
1 tsp soy sauce
3 oz (80 g, or a scant ½ cup) prepared sushi rice

1   Brush any dirt off the shiitake and remove the hard stems. Slice the mushrooms thinly.

2   Place all ingredients (except sushi rice) in a saucepan over medium heat. Bring to a boil, then turn the heat to low and simmer, stirring with cooking chopsticks from time to time, until all the liquid has evaporated.

3   Divide the rice, shape into 4 pieces, and arrange mushroom slices on each piece. Place the sushi on a serving dish.

Roasted Okra Nigiri-zushi

Boiling or sautéing works fine, but grilling okra until it is slightly charred really brings out the vegetable's sweetness. You can also briefly dip the okra in soy sauce before placing it on the rice. Choose okra pods that are bright green, with no brown spots, and be aware that larger pods may not be as tender as smaller ones.

Ingredients for 4 pieces:

4 medium okra pods, washed and patted dry, ends intact (1 oz / 30 g total)
3 oz (80 g, or a scant ½ cup) prepared sushi rice
prepared wasabi, to taste

1   Cut each okra pod in half lengthwise.

2   Place a roasting grill over a high flame. Roast the okra on it until the edges begin to brown.

3   Divide the rice and shape into 4 pieces. Spread a little wasabi on the flat side of each piece of okra and place on the rice. Arrange the sushi on a serving dish.

Simmered King Oyster Mushroom Nigiri-zushi

King oyster mushrooms, called *eringi* in Japanese, have a delicate aroma and an incredible texture, strongly reminiscent of the abalone served in the best sushi shops. These mushrooms will keep for as long as ten days if refrigerated in a paper bag.

Ingredients for 4 pieces:

1 large king oyster mushroom (2¾ oz / 80 g total)
1 Tbsp saké
½ tsp soy sauce
2 Tbsp water
3 oz (80 g, or a scant ½ cup) prepared sushi rice

1   Brush any dirt off the mushroom and remove the base of the stem. Cut the mushroom lengthwise into slices about ⅛ in (4 mm) thick.

2   Place the mushroom slices, saké, water, and soy sauce in a small pan over medium-high heat. Bring to a boil, then lower the heat and stir, turning mushrooms so they absorb flavor evenly, for 3 minutes or until the liquid has evaporated. Remove from heat.

3   Spread a bit of wasabi paste on one side of each mushroom slice. Divide the sushi rice and shape into 4 pieces. Place mushroom slices on top of each piece and arrange on a serving dish.

Braised Eggplant Gunkan-maki

Long and slender Japanese eggplant is ideal for this sushi, as it has a finer texture and is not as watery as globe eggplant. The eggplant tastes best when cooked until very soft. If there's not enough liquid in step 2, add a little water to the pan.

Ingredients for 4 pieces:

1 small eggplant (3½ oz / 100 g total)
4 Tbsp saké
1 tsp soy sauce
3 oz (80 g, or a scant ½ cup) prepared sushi rice
½ sheet dried nori, cut into four 7 x 1 in (19 x 3.5 cm) strips
¼ tsp grated ginger, or to taste

1   Cut eggplant lengthwise into slices about ¼ in (7 mm) thick.

2   Put the sliced eggplant, saké, and soy sauce into a small pan, cover, and place over medium-high heat. When steam begins to come out from under the lid, turn the heat to low and let steam for 4–5 minutes until the eggplant is soft and the liquid has been absorbed. Remove from heat and set aside, covered, to cool.

3   Divide the sushi rice and shape into 4 pieces. Wrap a strip of nori around each piece so that it encircles the rice, and use a grain of rice to stick the ends of the nori together. Place the topping on the rice and top with a dab of grated ginger.

Umeboshi Plum-and-Ginger-flavored Turnip Nigiri-zushi

The ginger adds a nice bite to this dish. If you prefer less heat, try grating the ginger instead of mincing it, or reducing the amount of ginger used.

It's important to use a mild white Japanese-style turnip in this recipe. European turnips are too coarse and strongly flavored to eat raw.

Ingredients for 4 pieces:

½ white turnip (kabu) (1¾ oz / 50 g total)
1 umeboshi plum
¼ tsp minced or grated fresh ginger
3 oz (80 g, or a scant ½ cup) prepared sushi rice

1   Cut the turnip into paper-thin slices. Remove the pit from the plum and break up the pulp with the back edge of a heavy knife.

2   Put the turnip slices and plum pulp into a small bowl. Add the ginger and mix well.

3   Divide the sushi rice and shape into 4 pieces. Arrange turnip slices on top of each piece and place on a serving dish.

Zucchini with Miso Gunkan-maki

The creamy taste of zucchini goes extremely well with the complex, salty flavor of red miso. For some reason, it takes on an almost cheesy taste, even though the ingredients include only vegetables. For a milder but still rich result, try using white miso.

Ingredients for 4 pieces:

¼ zucchini (1¾ oz / 50 g total)
½ Tbsp red miso
3 oz (80 g, or a scant ½ cup) prepared sushi rice
½ sheet dried nori, cut into four 7 x 1 in (19 x 3.5 cm) strips
¼ tsp grated fresh ginger, or to taste

1   Cut zucchini into paper-thin slices.

2   Use your hands to mix the zucchini and miso together in a small bowl, making sure the miso coats each slice. Put a plate or other flat object directly on the zucchini and place a heavy weight on top. Let stand for about 5 minutes.

3   Divide the sushi rice and shape into 4 pieces. Wrap a strip of nori around the circumference of each piece and use a grain of rice to stick the ends together. Place the topping on the rice and top with a dab of grated ginger.

Steamed Bell Pepper Nigiri-zushi

The colors of the peppers are so striking that I like to serve these for celebrations and special guests. The cooking time can be shortened if you prefer your peppers with a fresher flavor and more crunch.

Ingredients for 4 pieces:

¼ red bell pepper (1½ oz / 40 g total)
¼ yellow bell pepper (1½ oz / 40 g total)
2 Tbsp saké
pinch salt
1 tsp lemon juice
3 oz (80 g, or a scant ½ cup) prepared sushi rice

1   Cut each piece of bell pepper into thin strips.

2   Place the bell pepper strips, saké, and salt in a small pan over medium heat. Add lemon juice and cover. When steam begins to come out from under the lid, lower the heat and allow to steam for 2 minutes. Remove from heat and allow to cool.

3   Divide sushi rice and shape into 4 pieces. Arrange pepper strips on each piece of sushi, then place on a serving dish.

Sweet-and-sour Eggplant Nigiri-zushi

The luscious sweet-and-sour flavors go marvelously with the eggplant in this recipe. The sweetness is kept to a minimum here, so if you prefer a sweeter flavor, add a bit of sugar to the liquid.

Ingredients for 4 pieces:

1 small Japanese eggplant (2¾ oz / 80 g total)
3 Tbsp vinegar
2 Tbsp mirin
1 tsp soy sauce
3 oz (80 g, or a scant ½ cup) prepared sushi rice

1   Cut off and discard the calyx and bottom end of the eggplant, then slice thinly into rounds. Combine the vinegar, mirin, and soy sauce in a bowl. Add the eggplant and mix thoroughly. Let stand for at least 15 minutes.

2   Divide sushi rice and shape into 4 pieces. Gently squeeze the excess liquid from the eggplant slices and arrange on top of the rice. Place on a serving dish.

Fresh Tomato Gunkan-maki

At a glance, these look almost like gunkan maki made with tuna. They have a delightfully refreshing taste that really brings out the fruitiness of the tomato. For a different flavor, use a little salt and fresh basil instead of soy sauce.

Ingredients for 4 pieces:

½ small tomato (2½ oz / 70 g total)
½ Tbsp soy sauce
3 oz (80 g, or a scant ½ cup) prepared sushi rice
½ sheet nori, cut into four 7 x 1 in (19 x 3.5 cm) strips

1   Cut the tomato into ¼ in (7 mm) cubes. Place in a small bowl, add soy sauce, and mix well. Let stand for 5 minutes.

2   Divide the sushi rice and shape into 4 pieces. Wrap a strip of nori around the circumference of each piece, using a grain of rice to stick the ends together. Spoon tomatoes onto each piece, then arrange on a serving dish.

Japanese Leek with Lemon Gunkan-maki

This goes over well with fans of spicy food. If you prefer less heat, rinse the leek under cold water after slicing, then drain well before adding the lemon and salt.

If Japanese leeks are not available, use the white part of scallions or young leeks.

Ingredients for 4 pieces:

10 in (24 cm) length Japanese leek or two 8 in (20 cm) lengths
   Japanese leeks (2½ oz / 70 g total)
¼ tsp salt
1½ Tbsp lemon juice
3 oz (80 g, or a scant ½ cup) prepared sushi rice
½ sheet nori, cut into four 7 x 1 in (19 x 3.5 cm) strips

1   Cut the leek into 2 in (5 cm) lengths, then thinly slice each piece lengthwise to make fine strips. Put in a bowl, add the salt and lemon juice, and mix well. Let stand for 5 minutes.

2   Divide the sushi rice and shape into 4 pieces. Wrap a strip of nori around the circumference of each piece, using a grain of rice to stick the ends together. Top with the leek and arrange on a serving dish.

JAPANESE LEEK AND DRIED DAIKON CONSOMMÉ

This is a refreshing clear soup that doesn't use dashi stock. The dried daikon strips give the soup plenty of umami and sweetness, so dashi isn't necessary. If you substitute 2 tablespoons of miso for the salt and the soy sauce, you'll have a quick miso soup. If you can't find naganegi (Japanese long onion), use the white part of a young leek.

Ingredients for 2 servings:

2 Tbsp dried daikon strips (kiriboshi daikon)
7 in (18 cm) length naganegi, or one 5 in (13 cm) length young
   leek (1¾ oz / 50 g total)
1¼ cup (300 ml) water
1 Tbsp saké
¼ tsp salt
1 tsp soy sauce
chopped chives or scallions, for garnish

1   Wash the daikon strips and place them in a bowl with the water. When the daikon is soft (about 3 minutes), drain, reserving the soaking water for the soup stock, and cut into bite-sized pieces. Cut the onion into 2 in (5 cm) pieces, then slice each piece lengthwise to make matchsticks.

2   Place the onion and daikon with the soaking water in a saucepan over high heat and bring to a boil. Turn the heat to low and simmer for 3 minutes, then add saké, salt, and soy sauce, to taste. Remove from heat. Serve topped with chopped chives or scallion greens.

Simmered Japanese Leek Nigiri-zushi

Here the sweetness of the simmered leek or naganegi (Japanese long onion) and the sweet-and-sour soy sauce go perfectly with the sushi rice. You might want to cook larger portions of this and serve it as a side dish with rice, or a topping on tofu. If naganegi are not available, young leeks can be substituted.

Ingredients for 4 pieces:

1 small Japanese leek or young leek, washed, with roots and green part removed (3½ oz / 100 g total)
1 tsp soy sauce
2 Tbsp saké
½ tsp sesame oil
3 oz (80 g, or a scant ½ cup) prepared sushi rice

1   Cut the leek into 2 in (5 cm) pieces, then thinly slice each piece lengthwise into matchsticks.

2   Combine the leek, soy sauce, saké, and sesame oil in a covered saucepan over medium-high heat. When steam begins to come out from under the lid, lower the heat and steam for 5 minutes. When the leek is completely soft, remove from heat and allow to cool.

3   Divide the sushi rice and shape into 4 pieces. Arrange simmered leek on each piece and place on a serving dish.

Toasted Broccoli Nigiri-zushi

You may be surprised to find how delicious grilled broccoli is. The results are crunchier and more flavorful than when broccoli is boiled or steamed. A little dab of wasabi paste goes well with this, too.

Ingredients for 4 pieces:

½ head broccoli (3½ oz / 100 g total)
1 Tbsp lemon juice
¼ tsp salt
3 oz (80 g, or a scant ½ cup) prepared sushi rice
wasabi (optional)

1   Cut the broccoli stems lengthwise so that the florets can be pulled apart into bite-sized pieces.

2   Place a metal grill over a high flame. Roast broccoli, turning frequently, until it begins to brown.

3   Put the broccoli in a bowl with the lemon juice and salt and mix.

4   Divide the sushi rice and shape into 4 pieces. Arrange the broccoli on top, with a dab of wasabi if desired, and place on a serving dish.

Umeboshi Plum and Tororo Yam Gunkan-maki

I love tororo yam on rice, and I especially like eating it this way, in bite-sized pieces. The recipe calls for umeboshi plum, but you could also season it with a little shoyu or spice it up with some yuzukosho (citrus pepper paste) for variation in flavor.

Tororo yam (called *nagaimo* in Japanese) is available in many Asian markets. It is white with what looks like goosebumps on the surface. Japanese cooks use an *oroshi* grater (shown on p. 105), which has spikes rather than holes, to grind up the raw yam, but a very fine grater works just as well. Be aware that some people are sensitive to raw yam, and it makes their skin red and itchy. You should rinse your hands right away after grating the yam, just in case.

Ingredients for 4 pieces:

4 in (7 cm) length tororo yam (2¾ oz / 80 g total)
1 umeboshi plum
3 oz (80 g, or a scant ½ cup) prepared sushi rice
½ sheet nori, cut into four 7 x 1 in (19 x 3.5 cm) strips

1   Peel the yam and rinse under cold running water, then grate into a small bowl. Remove the pit from the umeboshi plum and break up the pulp with the back edge of a knife.

2   Mix the tororo yam and the umeboshi together.

3   Divide the sushi rice and shape into 4 pieces. Wrap a strip of nori around the circumference of each piece, using a grain of rice to stick the ends together. Spoon topping onto each piece, then arrange on a serving dish.

Turnip with Miso Gunkan-maki

Bruising and breaking the turnip into coarse pieces allows the flavor of the miso to be absorbed more efficiently than if the turnip is cut with a knife. It's best to make this topping just before serving, since the turnip will release moisture as it sits.

Be sure to use a mild Japanese-style white turnip (kabu) for this recipe. European turnips are too coarse and strongly flavored to eat raw.

Ingredients for 4 pieces

½ white turnip (1¾ oz / 50 g total), washed and trimmed
1 tsp red miso
¼ tsp shichimi pepper
3 oz (80 g, or a scant ½ cup) prepared sushi rice
½ sheet nori, cut into four 7 x 1 in (19 x 3.5 cm) strips

1   Cut the turnip into quarters.

2   Put turnip and miso into a plastic bag, add the shichimi pepper, and close tightly. Place on a solid surface. Use a rolling pin or other heavy implement to hit the turnip and break it into smaller pieces. Continue until the turnip is broken up and the ingredients are well blended.

3   Divide the sushi rice and shape into 4 pieces. Wrap a strip of nori around the circumference of each piece, using a grain of rice to stick the ends together. Spoon the turnips from the bag onto the sushi pieces. Arrange on a serving dish.

Shiitake Tempura Nigiri-zushi

Making the tempura coating with flour and soy milk gives this a very flavorful crunchiness. If you don't have soy milk, you can use water, which will make a thinner coating. In that case use a bit less flour.

Ingredients for 4 pieces:

4 fresh shiitake mushrooms (2 oz / 60 g total)
2 Tbsp flour
2 scant Tbsp plain soy milk
oil, for frying
salt to taste
3 oz (80 g, or a scant ½ cup) prepared sushi rice

1   Brush any dirt from the mushrooms and cut off the hard stems. Combine the flour and soy milk in a small bowl.

2   Pour about 2 in (5 cm) of oil in a deep, straight-sided frying pan and heat to 380°F (190°C). Dip the shiitake in the batter to coat thoroughly, then use tongs or cooking chopsticks to transfer to the hot oil. Cook, turning once or twice, until golden brown, about 3 minutes. Transfer to a paper towel–lined rack or plate and allow to drain.

3   Divide the sushi rice and shape into 4 pieces. Place a mushroom on top of the rice and sprinkle a bit of salt on each piece. Arrange on a serving dish.

Maitake Tempura Nigiri-zushi

The sushi rice is delicious when the soy sauce flavor seeps into it. Like all tempura dishes, tempura sushi is best when served hot.

Ingredients for 4 pieces:

3½ oz (100 g) maitake mushrooms
3 Tbsp flour
2½ Tbsp soy milk
oil, for frying
1 Tbsp soy sauce
1 Tbsp mirin
3 oz (80 g, or a scant ½ cup) prepared sushi rice

1   Remove the hard base from the maitake mushrooms and pull apart into bite-sized pieces. Combine the flour and soy milk in a small bowl.

2   Pour about 2 in (5 cm) of oil in a deep, straight-sided frying pan and heat to 380°F (190°C). Dip the maitake in the batter to coat thoroughly, then use tongs or cooking chopsticks to transfer to the hot oil. Cook, turning once or twice, until golden brown, about 3 minutes. Transfer to a paper towel–lined rack or plate and allow to drain.

3   Combine soy sauce and mirin in a small saucepan and bring to a boil. Remove from heat, and briefly toss the fried mushrooms in the mixture to coat.

4   Divide the sushi rice and shape into 4 nigiri pieces. Place fried maitake on top of each piece. Drizzle any remaining soy sauce–mirin mixture on top, then arrange on a serving dish.

Goya Teriyaki Nigiri-zushi

Goya is also known as bitter melon—and it is indeed bitter. To mellow the flavor, salt it after cutting, massaging the salt into the cut surfaces by hand. Then blanch it in boiling water for about 30 seconds before frying. You can also increase the amount of mirin to add sweetness.

Ingredients for 4 pieces:

⅓ goya, seeds and pith removed (2¾ oz / 80 g total)
½ Tbsp cooking oil
½ Tbsp mirin
½ Tbsp soy sauce
3 oz (80 g, or a scant ½ cup) prepared sushi rice

1   Halve the goya lengthwise, then slice each half into ⅛ in (4 mm) crescents.

2   Place the oil in a frying pan over medium heat. Add goya and sauté on both sides until browned. Add mirin and soy sauce, stir well to mix, and remove from heat.

3   Divide sushi rice and shape into 4 pieces. Place 2 or 3 goya crescents on each nigiri piece and arrange on a serving dish.

Roasted Eggplant Nigiri-zushi

This will always be one of my favorite kinds of sushi—the softness of the eggplant just goes so well with the sushi rice. You can vary the amount of ginger according to your palate. After drizzling on the soy sauce, add a few drops of sesame oil for extra richness.

Ingredients for 4 pieces:

1 small Japanese eggplant (2¾ oz / 80 g total)
3 oz (80 g, or a scant ½ cup) prepared sushi rice
1 tsp grated fresh ginger
soy sauce, to taste
sesame oil (optional)

1   Wash the eggplant but do not remove the calyx or base. Put the whole eggplant on a stovetop grill and roast slowly over a medium flame, turning occasionally, until the skin is blackened. Grate ginger.

2   Peel the eggplant while it is still hot. Cut in half crosswise, and then pull apart into bite-sized pieces.

3   Divide the eggplant into fourths. Divide the sushi rice and shape into 4 pieces. Place eggplant on the nigiri pieces, and top each with a dab of ginger and a little soy sauce. Add a few drops of sesame oil if desired. Arrange on a serving dish.

Roasted Cherry Tomato Gunkan-maki

Though there's nothing to this but tomatoes, roasted tomatoes have a unique depth of flavor, combining both sweetness and a smoky tang. You can enjoy the tomatoes just as they are, or add salt or soy sauce to broaden the flavor a bit.

Ingredients for 4 pieces:

6 cherry tomatoes
3 oz (80 g, or a scant ½ cup) prepared sushi rice
½ sheet dried nori, cut into four 7 x 1 in (19 × 3.5 cm) strips

1 Cut the cherry tomatoes in half. Place a dry frying pan over medium heat and arrange the cherry tomatoes in the pan in a single layer. Cook until tomatoes are browned and very soft. Remove from heat.

2 Divide the sushi rice and shape into 4 pieces. Wrap a strip of nori around the circumference of each piece, using a grain of rice to stick the ends together. Use a spoon to heap roasted tomatoes onto each piece, then arrange on a serving dish.

Miso-roasted Carrot Gunkan-maki

Charring the miso slightly is what gives this sushi its unique flavor, so don't remove the carrot from the heat until the miso is a little burnt. Any kind of miso will work, but I recommend that it not be too strong.

Ingredients for 4 pieces:

½ carrot (1¾ oz / 50 g total)
scant ½ Tbsp miso
3 oz (80 g, or a scant ½ cup) prepared sushi rice
½ sheet nori, cut into four 7 x 1 in (19 × 3.5 cm) strips

1 Cut carrot lengthwise into paper-thin strips.

2 Place a stove top grill over low heat and add the carrot strips. Cook slowly until they begin to brown on one side. Turn over and spread miso onto the browned surface. Continue to cook until miso begins to singe.

3 Divide the sushi rice and shape into 4 pieces. Wrap a strip of nori around the circumference of each piece, using a grain of rice to stick the ends together. Use a spoon to heap roasted carrots onto each piece, then arrange on a serving dish.

King Oyster Mushroom Steamed in Saké Nigiri-zushi

Although the mushroom will retain its chewy texture, it gets very juicy after steaming. There's just a bit of salt as flavoring, so serve it with soy sauce for dipping.

Ingredients for 4 pieces:

1 king oyster mushroom (2¾ oz / 80 g total)
1 Tbsp saké
pinch salt
prepared wasabi, to taste
3 oz (80 g, or a scant ½ cup) prepared sushi rice

1   Brush any dirt from the king oyster mushroom and remove the hard base of the stem. Slice lengthwise into 4 strips. Put in a bowl and sprinkle with saké and salt. Bring water to boil in a steamer and steam the mushroom slices for 3–4 minutes, then take them out of the steamer to cool.

2   Divide the sushi rice and shape into 4 nigiri pieces. Put a dab of wasabi on each slice of steamed king oyster mushroom, and place one on top of each nigiri piece. Arrange on a serving dish.

Carrot Steamed in Salt Nigiri-zushi

Rather than the usual wasabi, I pair this nigiri with mustard, which goes really well with the sweetness of the carrot. Don't dip it in soy sauce without tasting it first—it may be flavorful enough on its own.

Ingredients for 4 pieces:

½ carrot (1¾ oz / 50 g total)
¼ tsp salt
prepared karashi hot mustard, to taste
3 oz (80 g, or a scant ½ cup) prepared sushi rice

1   Cut carrot lengthwise into strips ⅛ in (5 mm) thick.

2   Sprinkle salt on carrot and massage by hand. Bring water to boil in a steamer and steam carrots for 5 minutes.

3   Divide the sushi rice and shape into 4 nigiri pieces. Put a dab of mustard on each steamed carrot slice and place a slice or two on top of each nigiri piece. Arrange on a serving dish.

Gingered Bamboo Shoot Nigiri-zushi

The soy sauce and saké give this a clean, fresh flavor, but if you'd prefer it to be slightly sweeter, add the same amount of mirin. For those who prefer less bite from the ginger, don't mince it—grate it.

Ingredients for 4 pieces:

½ **boiled bamboo shoot (3 oz / 80 g total)**
1¾ oz (50 ml) dashi stock (see p. 13)
2 tsp minced fresh ginger
2 tsp soy sauce
2 tsp saké
3 oz (80 g, or a scant ½ cup) prepared sushi rice

1 Cut the bamboo shoot lengthwise into ¼ in (7 mm) slices.

2 Combine the bamboo shoots, dashi stock, ginger, soy sauce, and saké in a pan over medium heat. Cover and bring to a boil. When steam begins to come out from under the lid, lower the heat and let simmer for 5 or 6 minutes, turning bamboo shoots occasionally. Remove from the heat and transfer to a bowl to cool.

3 Divide the sushi rice and shape into 4 pieces. Top each nigiri piece with a slice of simmered bamboo shoot.

Steamed Eggplant Gunkan-maki

This is just a wonderfully juicy, soft, luscious-tasting gunkan maki. The sauce calls for vinegar and ginger juice, but it tastes very nice with just soy sauce alone.

Ingredients for 4 pieces:

1 small Japanese eggplant (2¾ oz / 80 g total)
2 tsp vinegar
2 tsp soy sauce
1 tsp juice from grated fresh ginger
3 oz (80 g, or a scant ½ cup) prepared sushi rice
½ sheet nori, cut into four 7 x 1 in (19 x 3.5 cm) strips

1   Remove the calyx and bottom end of the eggplant. Cut lengthwise into ⅛ in (5 mm) thick strips. Bring water to boil in a steamer and steam for 5 minutes.

2   Combine vinegar, soy sauce, and ginger juice in a medium bowl. Add eggplant slices and toss to coat with the sauce while the eggplant is still hot.

3   Divide the sushi rice and shape into 4 pieces. Wrap a strip of nori around the circumference of each piece, using a grain of rice to stick the ends together. Spoon eggplant topping onto each piece of sushi, then arrange on a serving dish.

Steamed Enoki Mushroom Gunkan-maki

The enoki mushrooms have so much umami that a pinch of salt is truly all the extra flavor you need. If you really want more, just splash a few drops of soy sauce onto the finished sushi.

Ingredients for 4 pieces:

3½ oz (100 g) enoki mushrooms
pinch salt
3 oz (80 g, or a scant ½ cup) sushi rice
½ sheet nori, cut into four 7 x 1 in (19 x 3.5 cm) strips

1   Remove the hard base of the enoki mushrooms, and cut into 2 in (5 cm) lengths. Place in a heat-proof bowl and sprinkle with salt.

2   Bring water to boil in a steamer, put the bowl in, and steam the enoki for 3–4 minutes.

3   Divide the sushi rice and shape into 4 pieces. Wrap a strip of nori around the circumference of each piece, using a grain of rice to stick the ends together. Spoon the enoki mushrooms onto the sushi pieces. Arrange on a serving dish.

Pickled Napa Cabbage Nigiri-zushi

This recipe makes more pickles than you will need for the nigiri-zushi. The pickled cabbage will keep for 2 or 3 days in the refrigerator, so enjoy the leftovers on their own or with rice. A drop or two of soy sauce enhances their flavor.

Ingredients for 4 pieces:

3½ oz (100 g) napa cabbage (about 1½ cups when cut)
peel from ½ lemon
½ tsp salt
3 oz (80 g, or a scant ½ cup) prepared sushi rice

1   Wash the napa cabbage leaves and cut into bite-sized pieces. Cut lemon peel into thin strips.

2   Combine the napa cabbage, lemon peel, and salt in a heavy plastic ziplock bag. Massage all ingredients well by hand. Close the bag securely and refrigerate for at least an hour.

3   Divide the sushi rice and shape into 4 pieces. Top each nigiri piece with pickled cabbage, reserving the leftover pickles for another meal. Arrange nigiri on a serving dish.

Eggplant and Wasabi Nigiri-zushi

Feel free to adjust the amount of wasabi to suit your taste. The amount here is meant to give a bite to the nigiri, but if you'd prefer less heat, cut the amount in half. In this case, add a little more soy sauce to increase the flavor.

Ingredients for 4 pieces:

1 small Japanese eggplant (2¾ oz / 80 g total)
⅔ tsp prepared wasabi, or to taste
1 tsp soy sauce
3 oz (80 g, or a scant ½ cup) prepared sushi rice

1   Remove the calyx and base of the eggplant and slice into thin rounds. Blend the wasabi and soy sauce together, then combine with the eggplant in a heavy plastic ziplock bag. Massage the soy sauce into the eggplant by hand. Close the bag securely and allow to stand for at least 15 minutes.

2   Divide the sushi rice and shape into 4 pieces. Arrange marinated eggplant slices attractively on each nigiri piece. Place on a serving dish.

Simmered Shimeji Mushroom Gunkan-maki

Simmering the mushrooms in soy sauce gives them a wonderful aroma that goes very well with the sushi rice. It will save for 3 days or so refrigerated, so make more than you need to eat later with white rice or as a snack with some saké. Use brown buna-shimeji mushrooms if you can get them; otherwise, regular shimeji are fine.

Ingredients for 4 pieces:

3½ oz (100 g) shimeji mushrooms
½ Tbsp soy sauce
½ Tbsp saké
3 oz (80 g, or a scant ½ cup) prepared sushi rice
½ sheet nori, cut into four 7 x 1 in (19 x 3.5 cm) strips

1   Cut off the root mass at the base of the mushrooms. Pull the clusters apart into bite-sized pieces.

2   Combine the shimeji mushrooms, soy sauce, and saké in a saucepan over medium heat. Cover and bring to a boil. When steam begins to come out from under the lid, lower the heat and let simmer for 3–4 minutes, turning the mushrooms occasionally. Remove from heat and transfer to a bowl to cool.

3   Divide the sushi rice and shape into 4 pieces. Wrap a strip of nori around the circumference of each piece, using a grain of rice to stick the ends together. Use a spoon to heap simmered shimeji onto each piece, then arrange on a serving dish.

Simmered Shiitake and Umeboshi Plum Gunkan-maki

The shiitake flavor and the tartness of the plum give this gunkan-maki a very sophisticated taste. The topping also keeps well—about 3 days in the refrigerator—so make extra and imagine new uses for it, like mixing it with tofu. Delicious!

Ingredients for 4 pieces:

4 large fresh shiitake mushrooms (2 oz / 65 g total)
1 umeboshi plum
1 Tbsp saké
3 oz (80 g, or a scant ½ cup) prepared sushi rice
½ sheet nori, cut into four 7 x 1 in (19 x 3.5 cm) strips

1   Remove the hard stems from the shiitake and brush any dirt off the caps. Slice thinly. Remove the pit from the umeboshi plum and break up the pulp with the back edge of a knife.

2   Combine the shiitake, umeboshi, and saké in a saucepan over medium heat. Cover and bring to a boil. When steam begins to come out from under the lid, lower the heat and simmer for 2–3 minutes, or until the mushrooms are soft. Remove from heat and transfer to a bowl to cool.

3   Divide the sushi rice and shape into 4 pieces. Wrap a strip of nori around the circumference of each piece, using a grain of rice to stick the ends together. Heap simmered shiitake onto each piece, then arrange on a serving dish.

Savory Tofu Gunkan-maki

Children love the slightly sweet flavor of this gunkan maki. For a more piquant, "adult" taste, add a little amount of grated ginger. Either firm or soft tofu can be used, but "silken" tofu should be avoided, as it will not crumble properly.

Ingredients for 4 pieces:

⅓ block firm tofu (3½ oz / 100 g total)
2 tsp soy sauce
1 Tbsp mirin
3 oz (80 g, or a scant ½ cup) prepared sushi rice
½ sheet dried nori, cut into four 7 x 1 in (19 x 3.5 cm) strips

1   Put the tofu in a sieve or colander and allow to drain for about 10 minutes.

2   Place a small pan over medium heat. Add the tofu and sauté it, using cooking chopsticks or a spatula to crumble the tofu as it is heated.

3   When most of the water has evaporated from the tofu and the large pieces are broken up, add the soy sauce and mirin. Stir briefly to mix, then remove from heat and allow to cool.

4   Divide the sushi rice and shape into 4 pieces. Wrap a strip of nori around the circumference of each piece, using a grain of rice to stick the ends together. Spoon the tofu topping onto each piece of sushi, then arrange on a serving dish.

Seasoned Minced Eggplant Gunkan-maki

This amount of eggplant is easy to make, though it may be more than enough for 4 pieces. You can use it all to make 6 pieces of sushi, or eat the leftovers as a side dish with rice. It also makes a delicious topping for cold tofu.

Ingredients for 4 pieces:

1 small eggplant (3½ oz / 100 g total)
1 tsp grated fresh ginger
1 Tbsp soy sauce
1 Tbsp saké
1 Tbsp water
3 oz (80 g, or a scant ½ cup) prepared sushi rice
½ sheet dried nori, cut into four 7 x 1 in (19 x 3.5 cm) strips

1   Wash the eggplant, remove the stem, and mince the flesh coarsely.

2   Place the minced eggplant, grated ginger, soy sauce, saké, and water in a small covered pan over medium heat. When steam begins to come out from under the lid, lower the heat and let steam for 3–4 minutes, or until the eggplant is very soft. Remove from heat and allow to cool.

3   Divide the sushi rice and shape into 4 pieces. Wrap a strip of nori around the circumference of each piece, using a grain of rice to stick the ends together. Use a spoon to heap eggplant topping onto each piece, then arrange on a serving dish.

Roasted Bell Pepper Nigiri-zushi

To make really tasty roasted bell peppers, keep them over the flame until they blister. This really brings out the sweetness of the peppers and keeps them juicy, and the taste is just indescribable.

Ingredients for 4 pieces:

½ red or yellow bell pepper, quartered lengthwise and seeded (2½ oz / 75 g total)
prepared wasabi, to taste
3 oz (80 g, or a scant ½ cup) sushi rice

1   Place the pepper quarters skin-side-down on a stovetop grill. Roast both sides over a high flame until the skin begins to blister.

2   Divide the sushi rice and shape into 4 pieces. Smear a bit of wasabi on the underside of each pepper slice and place on the nigiri pieces. Arrange on a serving dish.

Roasted Cucumber Nigiri-zushi

Cucumbers are not usually roasted, which is a shame. They're just delicious! The crunchiness that remains complements the sushi rice perfectly.

Ingredients for 4 pieces:

½ Japanese cucumber (1¾ oz / 50 g total)
1 tsp rice vinegar
1 tsp soy sauce
3 oz (80 g) prepared sushi rice

1   Cut cucumber lengthwise into 4 long strips. Place on a stovetop grill over a high flame and roast, turning once, until the edges begin to singe. Remove from the heat and place in a bowl.

2   Mix together the vinegar and soy sauce. Pour the dressing over the cucumber and let marinate for 5 minutes.

3   Divide the sushi rice and shape into 4 pieces. Smear a bit of wasabi on the back of each cucumber strip and place on the nigiri pieces. Arrange on a serving dish.

Maki-Zushi

It's remarkable how something as simple as rolling up sushi rice and fillings in a sheet of nori can have such a compelling result. Delicious, pleasing to the eye, and easy to eat, maki-zushi has garnered fans all over the world, and for many, it is synonymous with "sushi." Everyone has their favorite (my daughter, for example, is particularly fond of kappa-maki cucumber roll), and it's easy to come up with new variations on the standard themes involving umeboshi plum, cucumber, or shiso. And since maki-zushi, unlike nigiri-zushi, has traditionally focused on vegetables, there are also plenty of classics to choose from.

If you're just starting out, stick to rolls with one or two fillings. Once you've mastered that, making plump futo-maki with multiple fillings is less daunting.

Deep-fried Vegetable and Abura-age Futo-maki-zushi

Rolling up these deep-fried vegetables makes for a delicious and surprisingly hearty meal. This sushi tastes great dipped in a little soy sauce; alternately, you can salt it lightly to bring out different flavors.

Ingredients for 1 roll:

2 ⅜ in (1 cm) strips abura-age (deep-fried tofu)
4 fresh shiitake mushrooms (2¼ oz / 65 g)
1 thin asparagus spear, about 7 in (19 cm) in length (1 oz / 30 g total)
2 in (5 cm) length carrot, cut from the wide end of the carrot (1 oz / 30 g total)
1 in (2 cm) wide daikon round, about 2 in (5 cm) in diameter
oil, for deep-frying
10½ oz (300 g, or 1½ cups) prepared sushi rice
1 sheet nori

1   In a frying pan with no oil, heat the abura-age strips until crisp.

2   Cut off the hard stem of the shiitake and slice the caps into thin strips. Slice the piece of carrot lengthwise into ⅜ in (1 cm) sheets, then cut each sheet to make four ⅜ in (1 cm) square bars. Remove the outer peel from the daikon and cut in half to make two ⅜ in (1 cm) rounds, then cut each round into four ⅜ in (1 cm) square bars.

3   Heat 2 in (5 cm) oil to 360°F (180°C) in a deep frypan. Pick up the daikon and carrot sticks with cooking chopsticks and place them carefully in the oil. Fry, turning from time to time with the chopsticks, until they are just brown around the edges. Do the same for the asparagus and the shiitake. Drain on a paper towel.

4   Assemble and roll the sushi using either a makisu or plastic wrap and a towel as described in the futo-maki instructions on p. 51. Cut the roll in half crosswise, then lay the halves side by side and cut into thirds, wiping the knife with a damp cloth after each cut. Arrange on a serving dish.

Marmalade Watercress Maki-zushi

The combination of sweet and sour flavors makes for a surprisingly tasty sushi roll. The slight bitterness of the marmalade complements the bite of the watercress nicely.

Ingredients for 1 roll:

1 bunch (2 oz / 60 g) watercress, washed
1 tsp marmalade
1 tsp soy sauce
½ sheet nori
3 oz (80 g, or a scant ½ cup) prepared sushi rice

1   Bring plenty of water to boil in a saucepan. Blanch the watercress for about 20 seconds, or until it turns bright green. Cool under running water and drain well.

2   Combine the marmalade and soy sauce in a bowl. Add the watercress and mix well by hand to coat.

3   Assemble and roll the sushi using either a makisu or plastic wrap and a towel as described in the hoso-maki instructions on p. 50. Cut the roll in half crosswise, then lay the halves side-by-side and cut into thirds, wiping the knife with a damp cloth after each cut. Arrange on a serving dish.

Chives and Umeboshi Plum Maki-zushi

photograh on page 48

If you have access to a Japanese market, try to find the long, mild asatsuki chives. Finely chopped banno-negi or naganegi can be used as well. Otherwise, regular chives or green onions work fine in this recipe.

Ingredients for 1 roll:

3 Tbsp finely chopped chives or green onions
1 umeboshi plum
3 oz (80 g, or a scant ½ cup) prepared sushi rice
½ sheet nori

1   Remove the pit from the umeboshi and break up the pulp with the back edge of a knife.

2   Combine the chives and plum pulp in a small bowl and mix with cooking chopsticks.

3   Assemble and roll the sushi using either a makisu or plastic wrap and a towel as described in the hoso-maki instructions below. Cut the roll in half crosswise, then lay the halves side-by-side and cut into thirds, wiping the knife with a damp cloth after each cut. Arrange on a serving dish.

How to Make Maki-zushi

If you have a makisu, it's very easy to make both thin (hoso-maki) and thick (futo-maki) rolls. Even if you don't have a makisu, you can use plastic wrap and a thin towel instead.

THIN MAKI-ZUSHI ROLLS (HOSO-MAKI)

1   Lay half a sheet of nori on the makisu and spread sushi rice on top. Use your hands to push the rice out to the edges on the left and right, leaving about ⅜ in (1 cm) uncovered on the top edge.

2   Lay the filling in a horizontal line on top of the rice (shown with cucumber in the photo). The upper boundary of the filling should be just below the center of the rice. You can smear a bit of wasabi on the rice next to the filling if you like.

3   Using the fingertips of both hands to keep the filling in place, lift the closest edge of the makisu with your thumbs, curling the nori and rice toward the line of filling.

4   Be sure that the edge closest to you remains parallel to the far edge as you roll the nori and rice in the direction of the filling.

5   As you begin to roll, squeeze the makisu around the nori to make a tight roll.

6   Continue rolling up the rice and nori in the makisu. Keep squeezing the makisu and pulling the roll toward you so it stays tight, using a light but firm touch.

7   When you reach the end of the roll, the free edge of the nori should stick to the nori on the outside of the roll. If it doesn't, wet your fingers lightly and dampen the free edge so it sticks.

8   Put the finished roll seam-side-down on a cutting board, giving it a final squeeze to fix the round shape, and remove the makisu. Wipe a sharp knife with a towel dampened in a water–vinegar solution. Cut the roll in half crosswise, then lay the halves next to each other and cut each into 3 pieces, wiping the knife after each cut. Arrange the sushi on a serving dish.

> If you don't have a makisu, spread out a piece of plastic wrap on a clean towel. Lay the nori on top of the plastic wrap, spread the rice on top, place the filling on the rice, and roll up in the towel as described above. This doesn't make quite as tight a roll as a makisu will, but it works pretty well.

THICK MAKI-ZUSHI ROLLS (FUTO-MAKI)

1 Lay one sheet of nori on a long makisu (one designed for futo-maki), and spread sushi rice on top. Use your hands to push the rice to  the left and right edges, leaving about 1¼ in (3 cm) of nori uncovered on the edge of the nori furthest from you. The rice at the upper edge, just before the bare nori, should be piled up a little higher to prevent the toppings from escaping as you roll the sushi.

2 Lay the fillings on the rice, one piece at a time. Start placing each type of filling in a horizontal line in the lower half of the rice rectangle, then lay the next filling in a line above it until the fillings reach the center line.

3 Using the fingertips of both hands to keep the topping in place, lift the nearest edge of the makisu with your thumbs, curling the rice and nori toward the fillings.

4 Be sure that the edge closest to you remains parallel to the far edge as you roll the nori and rice in the direction of the filling.

5 As you begin to roll, squeeze the makisu down and around the nori to make a tight roll.

6 Continue rolling up the rice and nori in the makisu. Keep squeezing the makisu and pulling the roll toward you so it stays tight, using a light but firm touch.

7 When you reach the end of the roll, the free edge of the nori should stick to the outside of the roll. If it doesn't, wet your fingers lightly and dampen the free edge so it sticks.

8 Put the finished roll seam-side-down on a cutting board, give it a final squeeze to fix the round shape, and remove the makisu. Wipe a sharp knife with a towel dampened in a water–vinegar solution. Cut the roll in half crosswise, then put the halves side by side and cut each into 3 pieces, wiping the knife after each cut. Arrange the sushi on a serving dish.

Classic Futo-maki-zushi

The recipes for koya-dofu in marinade and simmered shiitake mushrooms given below make larger amounts than you will need for futo-maki. Leftover koya-dofu can be eaten as-is for a side dish, chopped up and added to stir-fried vegetables, or rolled in cornstarch and deep-fried like chicken. Simmered shiitakes can also be eaten on their own as a side dish.

Ingredients for 1 roll:

1 square Koya-dofu in Marinade (see recipe below)
2 Simmered Shiitake Mushrooms (see recipe below)
1¾ oz (50 g, or a generous 1½ cups) spinach leaves, washed
  and trimmed
1 tsp soy sauce
1 tsp water
2 in (5 cm) length Japanese cucumber (1 oz / 30 g total)
½ medium carrot (1 oz / 30 g total)
9 oz (250 g, or 1⅓ cups) prepared sushi rice
1 sheet nori

1   Prepare Simmered Shiitake Mushrooms and Koya-dofu in Marinade (see recipes below). Slice mushrooms into thin slices.
      Lightly squeeze the liquid from 1 square of koya-dofu and cut into ⅜ in (1 cm) wide sticks.

2   Bring plenty of water to boil in a large saucepan. Blanch spinach for 30 seconds or until bright green, then remove with tongs and plunge into cold water (don't discard the boiling water yet). Squeeze out all the water and place spinach in a bowl. Combine soy sauce and water and pour over spinach. Toss well to cover, then squeeze the liquid from the spinach again. Cut the carrot into ⅜ in (1 cm) slabs, then cut lengthwise to make ⅜ in (1 cm) square bars. Simmer the carrots in the boiling water until tender. Quarter the cucumber lengthwise into sticks.

3   Assemble and roll the sushi using either a makisu or plastic wrap and a towel as described in the futo-maki instructions on p. 51. Put the filling ingredients on the rice in the following order: koya-dofu, shiitake, spinach, carrot, and cucumber.
      Cut the roll in half crosswise, then lay the halves side-by-side and cut into thirds, wiping the knife with a damp cloth after each cut. Arrange on a serving dish.

KOYA-DOFU IN MARINADE

This will keep for about 5 days if refrigerated.

5 squares koya-dofu (freeze-dried tofu)
2 cups (500 ml) dashi stock (page 13) or water
2 Tbsp saké
2 Tbsp mirin
2 Tbsp soy sauce
¼ tsp salt

1   Reconstitute koya-dofu by soaking in warm water for 5 minutes. Squeeze out the water by hand.

2   Put the koya-dofu in a saucepan and add the dashi, saké, mirin, soy sauce, and salt. Bring to a simmer over medium heat. Simmer, without allowing the liquid to boil, for 7–8 minutes. Remove from heat and allow to cool.

SIMMERED SHIITAKE MUSHROOMS

These will keep for about one week in the refrigerator.

6 dried shiitake mushrooms (1 oz / 30 g total)
1 scant cup (200 ml) water
1 Tbsp soy sauce
1 Tbsp saké

1   Reconstitute the dried shiitake mushrooms by soaking in warm water until soft. Squeeze out the water, remove stems and cut in thin slices.

2   Return to water, add soy sauce and saké, and simmer until liquid has almost evaporated. Remove from heat.

LETTUCE AND WAKAME SOUP

Ingredients for 2 servings:

1 or 2 leaves iceberg lettuce (1 oz / 30 g total)
1 Tbsp dried cut wakame
1 ¼ cups (300 ml) dashi stock (see p. 13)
1 Tbsp saké
pinch salt
1 tsp soy sauce

1   Stack the lettuce leaves, roll into a loose cylinder, and cut finely.

2   Put the dashi in a pan over medium-high heat. When it comes to a boil, add the lettuce and wakame and simmer briefly. Then add the saké, salt, and soy sauce. Remove from heat and serve.

California Roll

A California roll, with sesame-sprinkled rice on the outside and nori and fillings inside, looks impressive, but it's as easy to roll as regular futo-maki. Just be a little careful as you turn the nori over after spreading the rice on top. If tororo yam (nagaimo) is not available, try using sticks of jicama or Jerusalem artichoke for a similar juicy crunch.

Ingredients for 1 roll:

2 in (5 cm) length tororo yam
1 leaf green- or red-leaf lettuce (1 oz / 30 g total)
¼ avocado
2 in (5 cm) length Japanese cucumber
7½ oz (220 g, or 1¼ cup) prepared sushi rice
2 Tbsp white sesame seeds
1 sheet nori

1 Peel the tororo yam and rinse under cold running water. Slice lengthwise into ⅜ in (1 cm) wide slabs, then cut each sheet lengthwise to make four ⅜ in (1 cm) square bars. Cut or tear the lettuce into 4 long strips. Cut the avocado into ⅜ in (1 cm)-thick slices. Cut the cucumber lengthwise into four sticks.

2 Lay a piece of plastic wrap on a makisu or towel. Lay the nori on the plastic wrap and spread the sushi rice on top as described in the futo-maki instructions on p. 51. Sprinkle the sesame seeds evenly over the surface of the rice and press them into the rice with your fingertips.

3 Cover the rice with a second sheet of plastic wrap. Pick up the nori and rice, sandwiched between the two sheets of wrap, and carefully turn it over so that the nori is facing up. Remove the plastic on top of the nori.

4 Arrange the fillings on the nori and roll the sushi. Leaving the plastic wrap around the roll, cut it in half crosswise, then lay the halves side-by-side and cut into thirds, wiping the knife with a damp cloth after each cut. Remove the plastic wrap from each piece and arrange on a serving dish.

Asparagus and Umeboshi Plum Maki-zushi

The sweetness and the crunch of the asparagus make for a delicious hoso-maki. Be sure not to overcook the asparagus, though. As soon as it turns bright green, remove it from the water.

Ingredients for 1 roll:

1 stalk asparagus (1 oz / 30 g total)
1 umeboshi plum
½ sheet nori
3 oz (80 g, or a scant ½ cup) prepared sushi rice

1   Peel off the tough skin at the base of the asparagus. Remove the pit from the umeboshi plum and break up the pulp with the back edge of a knife.

2   Bring plenty of water to boil in a medium saucepan. Blanch the asparagus until it turns bright green, about 1 minute. Immediately remove from water and allow to cool. Place the asparagus and plum pulp in a bowl and use your hands to coat the asparagus with plum pulp.

3   Assemble and roll the sushi using either a makisu or plastic wrap and a towel as described in the hoso-maki instructions on p. 50. Cut the roll in half crosswise, then lay the halves side-by-side and cut into thirds, wiping the knife with a damp cloth after each cut. Arrange on a serving dish.

Pickled Cabbage Maki-zushi

The recipe makes 3 pickled cabbage leaves for the sake of convenience, but you only need 1 for the maki-zushi. Why not try eating the remaining pickles the Japanese way, accompanied simply by some white rice?

Ingredients for 1 roll:

3 leaves green cabbage (5¼ oz / 150 g total)
¼ cup (100 ml) water
1 Tbsp vinegar
1 Tbsp mirin
1 tsp salt
1 tsp soy sauce
1 dried red chili pepper
2 in (5 cm) square dashi konbu
3 oz (80 g, or a scant ½ cup) prepared sushi rice
½ sheet nori

1   Slice the chili pepper into thin rings. Cut the konbu into strips with kitchen scissors. Combine the water, vinegar, mirin, salt, soy sauce, chili pepper, and dashi konbu, and mix until salt is dissolved. Put the cabbage in a heavy plastic ziplock bag and add the vinegar mixture. Close the bag securely and refrigerate for at least 2 hours.

2   Using the cabbage leaf in place of a sheet of nori, assemble and roll the sushi using either a makisu or plastic wrap and a towel as described in the hoso-maki instructions on p. 50. Cut the finished roll in half crosswise, then lay the halves side-by-side and cut into thirds, wiping the knife with a damp cloth after each cut. Arrange on a serving dish.

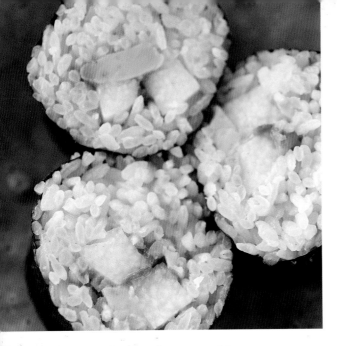

Avocado and Tororo Yam Futo-maki-zushi

The melt-in-your-mouth texture of the avocado goes wonderfully well with the crunchiness of the yams; what a great combination these two make! It's very tasty just the way it is, but you can always add a little wasabi and/or soy sauce if you wish.

Ingredients for 1 roll:

¼ avocado (2 oz / 60 g total)
1 tsp soy sauce
1 tsp lemon juice
2 in (5 cm) length tororo yam (nagaimo)
2 umeboshi plums
pinch salt
9 oz (250 g, or 1⅓ cup) prepared sushi rice
1 sheet nori

1   Slice the avocado thinly and place in a bowl with the soy sauce and lemon juice. Mix gently by hand, then let sit for 2–3 minutes. Peel the tororo yam and slice length-wise into ⅜ in (1 cm) slabs. Cut each slab lengthwise to make 4 bars that are ⅜ in (1 cm) square and 2 in (5 cm) long, and sprinkle them with salt. Remove the pits from the umeboshi plums and break up the pulp with the back edge of a knife.

2   Assemble and roll the sushi using either a makisu or plastic wrap and a towel as described in the futo-maki instructions on p. 51. Cut the roll in half crosswise, then lay the halves side-by-side and cut into thirds, wiping the knife with a damp cloth after each cut. Arrange on a serving dish.

Mashed Okra Maki-zushi

For this recipe, use two small okra pods or one big one. Trying to put too much filling in hoso-maki rolls makes them hard to roll up. If the sliminess of the okra makes it hard to work with, put it in a plastic bag with a corner cut off to make a ½ in (1 cm) opening, and squeeze the filling out onto the rice.

Ingredients for 1 roll:

2 small okra pods (½ oz / 15 g)
¼ tsp prepared wasabi
3 oz (80 g, or a scant ½ cup) sushi rice
½ sheet nori

1   Bring plenty of water to boil in a small saucepan. Blanch okra for 20–30 seconds. When cool, cut into small pieces, then crush to a coarse paste with the back edge of a heavy knife.

2   Combine the okra and wasabi in a small bowl and mix well.

3   Assemble and roll the sushi using either a makisu or plastic wrap and a towel as described in the hoso-maki instructions on p. 50. Cut the roll in half crosswise, then lay the halves side-by-side and cut into thirds, wiping the knife with a damp cloth after each cut. Arrange on a serving dish.

Deep-fried Vegetable Futo-maki-zushi

In this recipe, the vegetables are deep-fried without batter. The naganegi is cooked whole—don't slice it first. The sushi can be eaten as-is, or dipped in soy sauce or mentsuyu noodle sauce.

Ingredients for 1 roll:

3 small okra pods (1⅔ oz / 20 g total)
2 in (5 cm) length carrot
7 in (18 cm) length thin Japanese leek (1½ oz / 40 g total; use the white part of 1 or 2 green onions if naganegi is unavailable)
1 large king oyster mushroom (1¼ oz / 40 g)
oil for frying
9 oz (250 g, or 1⅓ cups) prepared sushi rice
1 sheet nori

1   Cut the stem end from the okra pods. Cut the carrot lengthwise into quarters. Brush any dirt from the king oyster mushroom, remove the hard base, and cut into quarters lengthwise.

2   Pour about 2 in (5 cm) of oil in a deep, straight-sided frying pan and heat to 380°F (190°C). Fry the vegetables in order, separately, each for about 1 minute. Remove while still bright in color.

3   Assemble and roll the sushi using either a makisu or plastic wrap and a towel as described in the futo-maki instructions on p. 51. Cut the roll in half crosswise, then lay the halves side-by-side and cut into thirds, wiping the knife with a damp cloth after each cut. Arrange on a serving dish.

Spinach with Sesame and Vinegar (side dish) recipe is on p. 102.

Cabbage Roll Maki-zushi

This recipe replaces the usual nori with cabbage. The stem vein running down the center of the leaf is very thick, so it should be trimmed down on the back side to a uniform thickness. Since the cabbage is already seasoned, you need only roll up the rice and cut it into pieces to eat.

Ingredients for 1 roll:

1 green cabbage leaf, 1¾ oz / 50 g total (it's easiest to use one of the outer leaves)
½ Tbsp soy sauce
4 oz (110 g, or a generous ½ cup) prepared sushi rice
1 Tbsp capers

1   Bring plenty of water to boil in a large saucepan. Trim the central stem vein of the cabbage so the leaf is of uniform thickness, then blanch for 2 minutes. Remove from heat and drain. Put cabbage in a bowl with the soy sauce, turn over several times to distribute the sauce evenly, and let stand for 3 minutes.

2   Chop the capers coarsely and mix into the sushi rice.

3   Using the cabbage leaf in place of a sheet of nori, assemble and roll the sushi using either a makisu or plastic wrap and a towel as described in the hoso-maki instructions on p. 50. Cut the finished roll in half crosswise, then lay the halves side-by-side and cut into thirds, wiping the knife with a damp cloth after each cut. Arrange on a serving dish.

Marinated Romaine Lettuce Maki-zushi

For the sake of convenience, this recipe makes more marinated lettuce than is needed for the sushi. You can use the leftover lettuce as a delicious accompaniment for rice, or mix it in with a salad for added flavor.

Ingredients for 1 roll:

⅜ cup (100 ml) water
1 Tbsp rice vinegar
1 tsp salt
1 tsp sugar
10 leaves romaine lettuce (3½ oz / 100 g total)
2 in (5 cm) square dashi konbu
2 pitted green olives in brine
4 oz (110 g, or generous ½ cup) prepared sushi rice

1   Combine water, vinegar, salt, and sugar in a mixing cup. Stir until salt and sugar are dissolved. Put the lettuce and konbu into a heavy plastic ziplock bag and add the vinegar mixture. Close the bag securely and refrigerate for at least 1 hour.

2   Drain olives, chop roughly, and mix into sushi rice.

3   Using two lettuce leaves in place of one sheet of nori, assemble and roll the sushi, either with a makisu or plastic wrap and a towel, as described in the hoso-maki instructions on p. 50. Cut the roll in half crosswise, then lay the halves side-by-side and cut into thirds, wiping the knife with a damp cloth after each cut. Arrange on a serving dish.

Oshi-zushi and Temari-zushi

In Japan, when we think of the styles of sushi known as *oshi-zushi* (pressed sushi) and *temari-zushi* (named after a traditional ball for tossing), we think of times of celebration such as New Year's and Girls' Day, or entertaining guests. One might think, therefore, that these types of sushi entail a lot of preparation or technique, but that is far from the case. One can, in fact, use plastic wrap and storage containers to make these very attractive shapes. They are also ideal to make with leftovers—even the smallest amount.

That's not to say that you shouldn't entertain with these. Large amounts are easy to make, quite satisfying, and much less trouble than cooking up a large meal with a similar kind of variety.

Glazed Carrot Temari-zushi

If the carrot slices are too coarsely cut they will overwhelm the sushi rice, so cut them fairly thin. This recipe keeps the flavoring simple with just a little salt. For a more aromatic flavor, you can add ¼ tsp or more yuzukosho (yuzu citron and green chili pepper) paste.

Ingredients for 3 temari-zushi balls:

½ **large carrot (1¾ oz / 50 g total)**
3 **Tbsp saké**
scant ¼ tsp salt
2 **Tbsp white sesame seeds**
4 **oz (110 g, or ¾ cup) prepared sushi rice**

1   Slice the carrot thinly into sheets, then stack slices and cut into thin slivers.

2   Place the carrot slivers, saké, and salt in a small saucepan over medium heat. Cook, stirring with cooking chopsticks, until the carrots are cooked through and glazed.

3   Remove carrots from heat and mix with sesame seeds, then allow to cool.

4   Divide the sushi rice and topping into thirds. Lay a piece of plastic wrap over your palm and spread a third of the carrot mixture on top. Place a third of the sushi rice on the carrots and shape into a ball as described in the instructions on p. 66. Repeat to make 2 more temari-zushi balls. Arrange on a serving dish.

Pickled Cucumber Temari-zushi see page 73

Balsamic-simmered Celery Oshi-zushi

This way of serving sushi really brings out the crunchy texture of the celery, and the balsamic vinegar adds a smooth acidity. Rice vinegar may be used in place of balsamic, but the amount should be reduced to 2 tsp since it is much more acidic.

Ingredients for 8 pieces (note that if you are using plastic containers to press the sushi, the number of pieces may vary):

1 large stalk celery (5 oz / 150 g total)
¼ tsp salt
1 tsp olive oil
1 Tbsp balsamic vinegar
11½ oz (330 g, or 1¾ cup) prepared sushi rice

1   Slice the celery thinly.

2   Put the celery, salt, olive oil, and balsamic vinegar together in a covered pan over medium-high heat. When steam begins to come out from under the lid, lower the heat and cook for 3 minutes or until just soft, removing the lid occasionally to stir with cooking chopsticks. Remove from heat and allow to cool.

3   Refer to the instructions for making oshi-zushi on page 65. Arrange the celery slices either in a wooden oshi-zushi mold or a flat-bottomed container lined with plastic wrap. Spread the sushi rice on top and gently press with the fingers to make a flat layer. Press the sushi in a wooden mold or plastic containers and slice as described in the instructions. Arrange on a serving dish.

Recipes continued on next page.

Roasted Tofu Temari-zushi

photograph on page 63

This is a very attractive temari-zushi with a piquant flavor. Make sure that you cook the tofu until all the liquid has evaporated; excess liquid will make the rice too soggy to hold together.

Ingredients for 3 temari-zushi balls:

⅓ block firm tofu (3½ oz / 100 g total)
2 umeboshi plums
4 oz (110 g, or a generous ½ cup) prepared sushi rice

1   Place the tofu in a strainer or colander and allow to drain for 5–10 minutes. Remove the pits from the plums and break up the pulp with the back edge of a knife.

2   Crumble the tofu into a frying pan over medium heat. Add the umeboshi pulp and cook, stirring with cooking chopsticks from time to time, until all the liquid has evaporated. Remove from heat and allow to cool.

3   Divide the sushi rice into thirds. Lay a piece of plastic wrap over your palm and arrange a third of the tofu mixture on top. Place a third of the sushi rice on the tofu and shape into a ball as described in the instructions on p. 66. Repeat to make two more temari-zushi balls. Arrange on a serving dish.

Vinegared Radish Temari-zushi

photograph on page 63

Using the vinegar mixture to season the sushi rice will add a slightly pinkish color and refreshing aroma. You can also use rice prepared this way for chirashi-zushi.

Ingredients for 3 temari-zushi balls:

10 red radishes, washed and trimmed (3½ oz / 100 g total)
2 tsp vinegar
1 tsp sugar
scant ¼ tsp salt
4 oz (110 g, or a generous ½ cup) warm cooked rice, not seasoned

1   Slice the radishes paper-thin and place in a medium-sized nonreactive bowl. Add the vinegar, sugar, and salt, mix well, and let stand for 5 minutes.

2   Strain the liquid to remove the radish slices, reserving the vinegar mixture. Gently cut the reserved mixture into the warm cooked rice to blend well.

3   Divide the sushi rice into thirds. Lay a piece of plastic wrap over your palm and arrange a third of the radish slices on top. Place a third of the sushi rice on the radishes and shape into a ball as described in the instructions on p. 66. Repeat to make 2 more temari-zushi balls. Arrange on a serving dish.

Salted Shiso Temari-zushi

photograph on page 63

When prepared in this manner, shiso leaves can be stored in the refrigerator for about a week. I like to prepare extra shiso. It's not only great for temari-zushi—you can also use it in place of nori for onigiri rice balls, or slice it up and serve it on top of chilled tofu.

Shiso—also called perilla, Japanese basil, or beefsteak plant—has a uniquely pungent, herbal zing. It really has no substitutes, but it is easy to cultivate. If you can't manage to buy it anywhere, you might consider growing your own.

Ingredients for 3 temari-zushi balls:

6 shiso leaves
¼ tsp salt, or to taste
½ tsp sesame oil, or to taste
4 oz (110 g, or a generous ½ cup) prepared sushi rice

1   Wash the shiso leaves and pat dry. Lay one leaf in a flat-bottomed container. Sprinkle a pinch of salt and a few drops of sesame oil over it. Then lay another leaf on top and repeat with the salt and sesame oil. Do the same for the remaining leaves. Allow to stand for at least 15 minutes; you can also cover the leaves and refrigerate them overnight or for longer periods.

2   Divide the sushi rice into thirds. Lay a piece of plastic wrap over your palm and arrange 2 shiso leaves on top. Place a third of the sushi rice on the leaves and shape into a ball as described in the instructions on p. 66. Repeat to make 2 more temari-zushi balls. Arrange on a serving dish.

How to Make Oshi-zushi

Making nigiri-zushi takes a little practice, but oshi-zushi is much more straightforward. The process, which uses a wooden mold, is simple, and it also makes a number of servings at once. If you don't have a traditional wooden oshi-zushi mold, you can make it using plastic food storage containers as described on the next page.

USING AN OSHI-ZUSHI MOLD:

1 Use a 10-to-1 water-vinegar mixture to wet the entire mold. Fit the long-slatted board in the bottom. Layer the topping ingredients on the bottom, covering it completely.

2 Scoop the sushi rice into the mold and press it down into an even layer over the topping. It should be about 2 in (5 cm) deep.

3 Cover the topping and rice with the shorter-slatted board. Be sure the wood is not dry.

4 Push down on the top board with even downward pressure, so that the rice is pressed into the topping.

5 Turn the mold upside down. Remove the long-slatted board that was previously on the bottom, exposing the topping.

6 Gently push the sushi "cake" up and out of the rectangular mold. The sushi will still be standing on the short-slatted pressing board that was originally on top. Carefully slide the sushi "cake" off the pressing board and onto a cutting board.

7 Dampen a cloth in the vinegar-water mixture and use it to wipe your knife before you cut the sushi into eight 1¼ in (3 cm) slices. Wipe the knife after each cut to keep the rice from sticking.

> NOTE: Some molds have grooves marking where to start the cuts for slicing the sushi "cake." If yours does as well, you can score the topping with a knife before removing the outer part of the mold in step 6. This will help you make evenly sized slices.

USING PLASTIC CONTAINERS:

1   Have ready two small or medium plastic food storage containers of the same size, preferably rectangular. Line one with plastic wrap.

2   Layer the topping into the plastic wrap–lined container so that it covers the bottom completely.

3   Scoop in enough sushi rice to make a layer about 2 in (5 cm) deep. Gently press with your fingers to make an even, flat layer. Cover the rice with a second piece of plastic wrap.

4   Place the other container on top so that the bottom is directly on top of the plastic wrap. Use both hands to push down on the top container with strong, even pressure so that the rice and toppings are firmly pressed together.

5   Remove the top container and the top layer of plastic wrap, and gently pull up on the bottom sheet of plastic wrap to remove the sushi "cake."

6   Handling the sushi "cake" carefully, place a lightweight cutting board on top of the rice, then invert the sushi so that the side with the topping faces up. Remove the plastic wrap.

7   Using a vinegar–water-dampened cloth to wipe the knife as described above, cut the sushi into slices. The size of the slices will depend on the size and shape of the plastic container you used, but they should be about 1½ oz (40 g) each.

How to Make Temari-zushi:

1   Place a square of plastic wrap on your left palm (or your right palm, if you are left-handed).

2   Lay the topping onto the plastic wrap, being sure to cover an area that is smaller than your palm.

3   Place about 1½ oz (40 g) sushi rice on the topping.

4   Curl your fingers up around the rice so it is surrounded with plastic wrap. Gather the plastic wrap together at the top, push out any air, and twist the wrap together, gently but firmly, to press the rice into a ball shape. Twist it three or four times, then slowly untwist and unwrap the temari-zushi ball. Place topping-side-up on a serving dish. You can reuse the plastic wrap to make the next ball.

Vinegared Lotus Root Oshi-zushi

This is also great to make in larger amounts. I sometimes serve the lotus roots alone as a dish to go along-
side rice. The flavoring is very simple—vinegar and
sugar—but just a bit of salt or some finely minced ginger are good additions.

Ingredients for 8 pieces:

8 shiso leaves
½ large lotus root (4 oz / 120 g total)
3 Tbsp vinegar
2 tsp sugar
11½ oz (330 g, or 1¾ cups) prepared sushi rice

1   Wash the shiso leaves, pat dry, and mince finely. Scrub
the lotus root well and slice thinly. Bring plenty of water
to a boil in a saucepan and blanch the lotus for about 1
minute. When it looks shiny and transparent, remove from
heat, drain, and put in a small bowl to cool.

2   Mix the vinegar and sugar together until the sugar
dissolves. Add to the lotus root and mix well by hand. Let
stand for more than 5 minutes.

3   Put the sushi rice in a bowl. Add the minced shiso
leaves and mix gently.

4   Refer to the instructions for making oshi-zushi on
page 65. Arrange the lotus root either in a wooden oshi-
zushi mold or a flat-bottomed container lined with plastic
wrap. Spread the sushi rice on top and gently press with
the fingers to make a flat layer. Press the sushi in a wooden
mold or plastic containers and slice as described in the
instructions. Arrange on a serving dish.

Umeboshi Plum and Cabbage Oshi-zushi

Blending the cabbage with the umeboshi plums gives it a nice pickled flavor—this makes a good side dish just on its own. You can also leave out the cabbage and make it with just the plums and seasoned sushi rice.

Ingredients for 8 pieces:

5 large umeboshi plums
3 green cabbage leaves (5¼ oz / 150 g total)
11½ oz (330 g, or 1¾ cups) prepared sushi rice

1   Remove the pits from the umeboshi plums. Break up the pulp by hitting it with the back edge of a knife. Blend half of the plum pulp into the rice.

2   Coarsely chop or tear the cabbage leaves and put them in a bowl. Massage the remaining plum pulp into the cabbage leaves. Allow to stand for 5 minutes, then tilt the bowl over the edge of the sink and squeeze out any expelled moisture from the cabbage leaves.

3   Refer to the instructions for making oshi-zushi on page 65. Place the cabbage in either a wooden oshi-zushi mold or a flat-bottomed container lined with plastic wrap. Spread the sushi rice on top and gently press with the fingers to make a flat layer.

4   Press to make oshi-zushi and slice. Arrange on a serving dish.

Spinachi Hitashi (side dish) recipe is on p. 102

Mustard-flavored Cabbage Temari-zushi

The hot and sour mustard taste goes great with the cabbage, and surprisingly well with the sushi rice. This dish has a Western feel, and I find it also goes well with beer or wine.

Ingredients for 3 temari-zushi balls:

3 small cabbage leaves (use the outer leaves from a small head of cabbage) (4 oz / 120 g total)
½ Tbsp soy sauce
½ Tbsp whole-grain mustard
4 oz (110 g, or a generous ½ cup) prepared sushi rice

1 Bring plenty of water to a boil in a large saucepan. Cut the thickest part of the central vein from each cabbage leaf, then blanch, for 1–3 minutes—until the leaves become soft. Remove from heat and drain well.

2 Mix the soy sauce and mustard in a bowl, then add the cabbage. Massage the sauce into the leaves, then let stand for about 5 minutes.

3 Divide the sushi rice into thirds. Lay a piece of plastic wrap over your palm and arrange a cabbage leaf on top—work near a sink, as the sauce can get pretty drippy. Place a third of the sushi rice on the cabbage and shape into a ball as described in the instructions on p. 66. Repeat to make 2 more temari-zushi balls. Arrange on a serving dish.

Simmered Cucumber and Umeboshi Plum Oshi-zushi

The tartness of the plum and the light taste of the cucumber make this a perfect dish for midsummer, when appetites tend to shrink. For even more zest, add a bit of grated ginger to the simmered ingredients.

Ingredients for 8 pieces:

1 Japanese cucumber (3½ oz / 100 g total)
1 large umeboshi plum
11½ oz (330 g, or 1¾ cups) prepared sushi rice

1   Cut off the ends of the cucumber and cut crosswise to the width of your mold. Slice the pieces lengthwise into ⅛ in (4 mm) thick strips. Remove the pits from the umeboshi plums and break up the pulp with the back edge of a knife.

2   Combine the cucumber and umeboshi in a saucepan. Barely cover with water and bring to a boil, then turn heat to low and let simmer for about 5 minutes. Continue cooking until the liquid has evaporated.

3   Refer to the instructions for making oshi-zushi on page 65. Place the cucumbers in either a wooden oshi-zushi mold or a flat-bottomed container lined with plastic wrap. Spread the sushi rice on top and gently press with the fingers to make a flat layer. Make oshi-zushi and slice as described in the instructions. Arrange on a serving dish.

Simmered Carrot and Mandarin Orange Oshi-zushi

The tang and sweetness of the mandarin orange juice lessen the amount of vinegar and sugar needed in the rice. Using segments of mandarin orange as a garnish for this sushi adds a nice touch.

Ingredients for 8 pieces:

pulp of 1 small mandarin orange, (3 Tbsp total)
1 tsp sugar
½ tsp salt
1 Tbsp vinegar
11½ oz (330 g, or 1¾ cups) warm cooked rice, not seasoned
1 medium carrot (3½ oz / 100 g total)
2 Tbsp mirin
2 Tbsp saké
2 tsp soy sauce

1 Peel the carrot and cut into 2 in (5 cm) lengths. Slice each piece lengthwise into sheets ⅛ in (5 mm) thick.

2 Combine the carrot, mirin, saké, and soy sauce in a covered saucepan over medium-high heat. When steam begins to come out from under the lid, reduce the heat and steam for 4–5 minutes, or until carrots are soft. Remove from heat and allow to cool.

3 Combine the mandarin orange, sugar, salt, and vinegar and mix well. Cut gently into the warm rice to make mandarin orange sushi rice.

4 Refer to the instructions for making oshi-zushi on page 65. Arrange the carrot slices on either a wooden oshi-zushi mold or a flat-bottomed container lined with plastic wrap. Spread the sushi rice on top and gently press with the fingers to make an even surface. Press to make oshi-zushi and slice as described in the instructions. Arrange on a serving dish, garnishing with fresh mandarin orange sections.

Pickled Zucchini Temari-zushi

This recipe calls for larger amounts so that the pickles will be easy to make. One delicious way to deal with the leftovers is simply to drizzle olive oil on them and dig in.

Ingredients for 3 temari balls:

1 small zucchini (5¼ oz / 150 g total)
2 in (5 cm) square dashi konbu
2 Tbsp water
1 tsp sugar
1 tsp salt
1 tsp soy sauce
1 Tbsp lemon juice
2 Tbsp grapefruit juice
4 oz (110 g, or a generous ½ cup) prepared sushi rice

1   Cut zucchini into thin slices. Cut dashi konbu into thin strips with kitchen scissors.

2   Combine the water, sugar, salt, soy sauce, lemon juice, grapefruit juice, and dashi konbu in a bowl and stir until the salt is dissolved. Put the zucchini into a heavy plastic ziplock bag, pour the liquid over, and seal securely. Refrigerate for at least an hour.

3   Divide the sushi rice into thirds. Lay a piece of plastic wrap over your palm and place several zucchini slices on top. Place a third of the sushi rice on the zucchini and shape into a ball as described in the instructions on p. 66. Repeat to make 2 more temari-zushi balls. Arrange on a serving dish.

Pickled Cucumber Temari-zushi

These cucumber pickles keep well in the refrigerator. They make a great addition to a salad with lettuce, daikon radish, and other raw vegetables.

Ingredients for 3 temari balls:

2 Japanese cucumbers (7 oz / 200 g total)
3 Tbsp (50 ml) water
1 Tbsp vinegar
1 Tbsp mirin
1 scant tsp salt
1 tsp sesame oil
2 in (5 cm) square dashi konbu
4 oz (110 g, or a generous ½ cup) prepared sushi rice

1   Cut cucumber into thin slices. Cut dashi konbu into thin strips with kitchen scissors.

2   Combine water, vinegar, mirin, salt, konbu, and sesame oil in a bowl and mix until salt is dissolved. Place the cucumbers in a heavy plastic ziplock bag and pour the liquid over. Seal securely and refrigerate for at least an hour.

3   Divide the sushi rice into thirds. Lay a piece of plastic wrap over your palm and place several cucumber slices on top. Place a third of the sushi rice on the cucumber and shape into a ball as described in the instructions on p. 66. Repeat to make two more temari-zushi balls. Arrange on a serving dish.

Pickled Carrot Temari-zushi

This pickled carrot also is delicious sautéed with cabbage and onion.

Ingredients for 3 temari balls:

2 medium carrots (5¼ oz, or 150 g)
3 Tbsp water
1 Tbsp vinegar
1 Tbsp mirin
½ tsp salt
¼ tsp yuzukosho paste
2 in (5 cm) square of dashi konbu
4 oz (110 g, or a generous ½ cup) sushi rice

1   Cut the carrot into 2 in (5 cm) long pieces, then slice each piece into thin sheets. Cut the dashi konbu into thin strips using kitchen scissors.

2   Combine water, vinegar, mirin, salt, yuzukosho paste, and dashi konbu and stir until the salt is dissolved. Place the carrot in a sturdy plastic bag ziplock bag, pour the liquid over, and seal securely. Refrigerate for at least an hour.

3   Divide the sushi rice into thirds. Lay a piece of plastic wrap over your palm and place several carrot slices on top. Place a third of the sushi rice on the carrot and shape into a ball as described in the instructions on p. 66. Repeat to make two more temari-zushi balls. Arrange on a serving dish.

Gingered Turnip Oshi-zushi

The sushi rice here is seasoned with a mixture of mirin, vinegar, and ginger, so it is not as sweet as typical sushi. The turnip is also delightful when used to make temari-zushi.

Ingredients for 8 pieces:

1 large Japanese turnip (kabu) (5¼ oz / 150 g total)
½ tsp salt
1½ Tbsp vinegar
1½ Tbsp mirin
½ tsp grated ginger
11½ oz (330 g, or 1¾ cups) cooked rice, not seasoned

1   Cut turnip into paper-thin rounds and put in a bowl. Sprinkle with salt, massage by hand for 1–2 minutes and squeeze out excess water. Add vinegar, mirin, and ginger, stir well to combine, and let stand for at least 15 minutes.

2   Stir the turnip mixture well and measure out 2 Tbsp of the liquid. Sprinkle over the warm cooked rice and toss gently to make sushi rice.

3   Refer to the instructions for making oshi-zushi on page 65. Arrange the turnip slices in either a wooden oshi-zushi mold or a flat-bottomed container lined with plastic wrap. Spread the sushi rice on top and gently shape into a uniform layer with fingers. Press to make oshi-zushi and slice as described in the instructions. Arrange on a serving dish.

Pickled Cucumber Oshi-zushi

Like the gingered turnip oshi-zushi, this recipe also uses liquid from the pickling to make the sushi rice. This gives the rice a faint hint of cucumber, which is very refreshing.

Ingredients for 8 pieces:

1 Japanese cucumber (3½ oz / 100 g total)
½ tsp salt
2 Tbsp vinegar
2 tsp mirin
11½ oz (330 g, or 1¾ cups) cooked rice, not seasoned

1   Cut cucumber into thin rounds and place in a bowl. Sprinkle with salt, massage for a minute by hand, then let stand for 3 minutes. Tilt the bowl over the edge of the sink and squeeze out excess water.

2   Sprinkle vinegar and mirin on cucumber, mix well, and let stand for 5 minutes.

3   Mix the cucumber pickles once more, then pour off the liquid into a small bowl or measuring cup. Mix the liquid with the unseasoned cooked rice to make sushi rice.

4   Refer to the instructions for making oshi-zushi on page 65. Arrange the cucumber in either a wooden oshi-zushi mold or a flat-bottomed container lined with plastic wrap. Spread the sushi rice on top and gently shape into a uniform layer with fingers. Press to make oshi-zushi and slice as described in the instructions. Arrange on a serving dish.

Umeboshi-pickled Onion
Oshi-zushi

If you wish to soften the sharp taste of the onion, add a pinch of salt after slicing, mix well, and let sit for 3 minutes. Rinse well under cold running water, squeeze out excess water, and the harshness will disappear.

Ingredients for 8 pieces:

⅓ **large yellow onion (2¾ oz / 80 g total)**
2 umeboshi plums
11½ oz (330 g, or 1¾ cups) prepared sushi rice

1   Slice the onion paper-thin. Salt and rinse as described above if desired. Remove the pit from the umeboshi plum. Break up the pulp with the back edge of a knife.

2   Mix the onion and umeboshi plum in a shallow bowl large enough for a plate to fit inside. Lay a plate directly on the onion mixture and place a weight or water-filled container on top. Let stand for 15 minutes to remove excess moisture, then tilt the bowl over the edge of the sink and squeeze out the expelled liquid from the onions by hand.

3   Refer to the instructions for making oshi-zushi on page 65. Arrange the onion in either a wooden oshi-zushi mold or a flat-bottomed container lined with plastic wrap. Spread the sushi rice on top and gently shape into a uniform layer with fingers. Press to make oshi-zushi and slice as described in the instructions. Arrange on a serving dish.

KOMATSUNA AND GRATED DAIKON

I love the fact that something as simple as this makes such a wonderful side dish. You can replace the vinegar in the marinade with juice from a sudachi citrus if you can get it; this adds a more refined taste.

Ingredients for 2 servings:

½ **bunch komatsuna greens (3½ oz / 100 g total)**
1¼ in (3 cm) length daikon (3½ oz / 100 g total)
1 tsp + 1 Tbsp soy sauce
1 tsp dashi stock or water
1 Tbsp vinegar

1   Bring plenty of water to a boil in a medium saucepan. Have a bowl of cold water ready in the sink. Blanch the komatsuna for 1 minute, then plunge into the cold water. Drain and squeeze out the water, then cut into bite-sized pieces. Peel the daikon and grate on a daikon-oroshi or fine grater.

2   Mix together 1 tsp of the soy sauce and 1 tsp water or dashi. Sprinkle the komatsuna with this mixture, then thoroughly squeeze out liquid.

3   Combine the grated daikon, vinegar, and 1 Tbsp soy sauce in a bowl and mix gently. Add the komatsuna and mix again. Transfer to a serving dish.

Roasted Shiitake Temari-zushi

Grilling the mushrooms until they are slightly charred really brings out the aromatic flavor, and biting into them releases a delightful juiciness. This very simple recipe calls only for soy sauce as seasoning, but feel free to add a squeeze of lemon juice for more flavor.

Ingredients for 3 temari balls:

9 small fresh shiitake mushrooms (4½ oz / 120 g)
1 tsp soy sauce
4 oz (110 g, or a generous ½ cup) prepared sushi rice

1   Remove the hard stems from the shiitake at the base of the cap and brush off any dirt. Place on a stovetop grill over low heat and grill, turning from time to time, until the edges singe. Remove from heat and place in a bowl. Drizzle soy sauce over and toss to coat.

2   Divide the sushi rice into thirds. When the shiitake are cool enough to handle comfortably, lay a piece of plastic wrap over your palm and lay 3 shiitake on top, stem-side-down. Place a third of the sushi rice on the shiitake and shape into a ball as described in the instructions on p. 66. Repeat to make 2 more temari-zushi balls. Arrange on a serving dish.

Braised Turnip Temari-zushi

After adding the soy sauce, leave the heat on so the soy sauce gets a little scorched. The faint bitterness blends very well with the sushi rice, and stimulates the appetite. A Japanese-style white turnip (kabu) is best for this recipe.

Ingredients for 3 temari balls:

⅔ small white turnip, trimmed (2½ oz / 70 g total)
1 tsp sesame oil
1½ tsp soy sauce
4 oz (110 g, or a generous ½ cup) prepared sushi rice

1   Cut turnip into ⅛ in (4 mm) thick slices.

2   Heat sesame oil in frying pan over medium heat. Add turnips in a single layer and sauté until brown. Turn once and brown the other side. Drizzle with soy sauce, stir to mix well, and leave on heat until the soy sauce begins to singe. Remove from heat immediately and allow to cool.

3   Divide the sushi rice and turnip slices into thirds. When the turnips are cool enough to handle comfortably, lay a piece of plastic wrap over your palm and spread a third of the turnips on top, layering them attractively. Place a third of the sushi rice on the turnips and shape into a ball as described in the instructions on p. 66. Repeat to make 2 more temari-zushi balls. Arrange on a serving dish.

Lemon-roasted Japanese Leek Temari-zushi

Some people—especially children—don't like the flavor of wasabi. You can always leave the wasabi out of the main topping and sprinkle it over the temari ball after serving.

Leeks or long Japanese naganegi onions can be used in this recipe; if they are not available, use the white part of some plump green onions.

Ingredients for 3 temari balls:

3½ in (9 cm) length Japanese leek or young leek (3½ oz / 100 g total; use the bottom part)
½ Tbsp lemon juice
½ Tbsp soy sauce
¼ tsp prepared wasabi, or to taste
4 oz (110 g, or a generous ½ cup) prepared sushi rice

1   Remove the roots and tough outer layers of the leek and cut into thirds. Cut each third in half lengthwise.

2   Place the leek halves on a stovetop grill and roast over a low flame, turning occasionally, until soft and browned at the edges. Remove from heat. Combine the lemon juice, soy sauce, and wasabi in a bowl. Add the roasted leeks and mix well.

3   Divide the sushi rice and topping into thirds. Lay a piece of plastic wrap over your palm and place a third of the leeks on top. Place a third of the sushi rice on the leeks and shape into a ball as described in the instructions on p. 66. Repeat to make two more temari-zushi balls. Arrange on a serving dish.

Chirashi-zushi, Maze-zushi, and Inari-zushi

These three types of sushi aren't as well known in other countries as nigiri-zushi and maki-zushi, but they are big favorites in Japan. Making them is a simple matter of quickly mixing ingredients into sushi rice (maze-zushi), sprinkling the ingredients on top (chirashi-zushi), or stuffing the rice into sweet pouches of deep-fried tofu (inari-zushi). Maze-zushi and chirashi-zushi are especially accessible for beginners.

Children of all ages love inari-zushi. All you have to do is season the abura-age (deep-fried tofu pouches) and fill them with sushi rice. If you keep the seasoned abura-age pouches in the freezer, you can use them anytime.

Citrus, Lotus Root, and Mushroom Chirashi-zushi

If *natsu-mikan*, a very tart variety of citrus, is unavailable, grapefruit works equally well. (A ruby grapefruit adds an especially colorful accent!) No matter what kind of citrus you use, the refreshing aroma of the sushi rice makes this chirashi-zushi a unique treat.

Ingredients for 2 servings:

½ small lotus root (2¾ oz / 80 g total)
4 button mushrooms (2¾ oz / 80 g total)
4 thin spears asparagus (4¼ oz / 120 g total)
½ natsu-mikan or grapefruit
2 Tbsp white sesame seeds
11½ oz (330 g, or 1½ cups) warm cooked rice, not seasoned
1½ Tbsp juice from a natsu-mikan or grapefruit
½ tsp sugar
2 tsp rice vinegar
½ tsp salt

1　Bring plenty of water to boil in a medium saucepan. Scrub the lotus root and slice it into thin rounds. Stack the rounds and cut crosswise into quarters. Blanch in the boiling water for 1 minute. Brush any dirt off the mushrooms, cut off the base of the stem, and slice thinly. Blanch for 30 seconds. Peel the citrus and divide it into sections, then remove the thin membrane that surrounds each segment. Combine the blanched lotus root and mushrooms with the citrus flesh and sesame seeds in a bowl.

2　Mix the citrus juice, sugar, vinegar, and salt in a measuring cup until the salt is dissolved. Scoop the rice into a wooden sushi tub or large bowl, then incorporate the juice mixture with a cutting, tossing motion to season the rice. Add the remaining ingredients and mix gently until well blended. Scoop the finished chirashi into a serving dish.

How to Make Chirashi-zushi and Maze-zushi

1   Have a wooden sushi tub or large bowl ready. Refer to the instructions on p. 12 to make sushi rice, and allow the rice to cool to room temperature as you prepare your other ingredients.

2   For maze-zushi, quickly and gently mix the prepared ingredients into the sushi rice. For chirashi-zushi, fill the serving dish with

sushi rice and arrange the prepared ingredients on top to look as appetizing as possible.

How to make Inari-zushi

Ingredients for 8 inari pouches:

4 rectangular sheets abura-age (deep-fried tofu)
4 Tbsp saké
2 Tbsp soy sauce
2 Tbsp mirin
3 oz (100 ml) water
15½ oz (440 g, or 2⅓ cups) prepared sushi rice

1   Bring plenty of water to boil in a large saucepan. Blanch the abura-age in boiling water for 30 seconds and drain well. When cool enough to touch,

squeeze out the water by hand, then cut each rectangle in half so that you have 8 square inari pouches.

2   Combine the inari pouches, saké, soy sauce, mirin, and water in a saucepan over medium heat. Bring to a simmer and let cook for about

10 minutes. Remove from heat and let the pouches sit for 10–15 minutes to absorb the liquid.

3   Remove the inari pouches from the pan and gently squeeze out excess liquid so they don't drip (but don't squeeze them dry, as you want some of the liquid to soak into the rice inside).

4   To fill the pouches, divide the sushi rice into eighths. Dampen your hand with vinegar water and pick up one portion of rice. Squeeze the rice gently so it sticks together, and place it inside the inari pouch.

5   Tuck one of the open flaps of the inari pouch inside the other to close the pouch. Arrange the inari-zushi open-side-down on a serving dish.

Shiitake Steamed with Umeboshi Plum Maze-zushi

This dish showcases the tartness of the umeboshi plum and the sweetness of the mirin. It's actually more of a normal rice dish than a typical sushi dish, but the rich flavor makes for a delicious meal on its own.

Ingredients for 2 servings:

8 fresh shiitake mushrooms (4¼ oz / 120 g total)
3 large umeboshi plums
2 Tbsp mirin
2 or 3 Tbsp finely chopped chives
11½ oz (330 g, or 1¾ cups) cooked rice, not seasoned

1   Brush any dirt from the shiitake and remove the hard stems, then cut into thin slices. Remove the pits from the plums and break up the pulp with the back edge of a knife.

2   Combine the shiitake slices and umeboshi pulp in a heat-proof bowl. Add the mirin and mix briefly. Bring water to boil in a steamer and steam the shiitake mixture in the bowl for 3 minutes.

3   Mix the mushrooms, liquid and all, into the cooked rice. Put into serving dish and top with chopped chives.

Pickled Radish and Cucumber Maze-zushi

The vinegar–marinated radish and cucumber give the rice its flavor in this extremely simple maze-zushi. The radish also lends a beautiful pink tinge to the rice.

Ingredients for 2 servings:

7 red radishes (2½ oz / 70 g total)
⅔ Japanese cucumber (2½ oz / 70 g total)
1 Tbsp mirin
1⅔ Tbsp rice vinegar
½ tsp salt
11½ oz (330 g, or 1¾ cups) warm cooked rice, not seasoned

1   Thinly slice radishes and cucumber. Combine the mirin, vinegar, and salt in a bowl, and stir to dissolve the salt. Add the radishes and cucumber, mix, and let stand for 4–5 minutes.

2   Add the warm cooked rice to the bowl and mix gently until all ingredients are combined. Transfer to a serving dish.

Shiitake and Green Spring Onion Maze-zushi

The combination of the onions and the shiitake mushrooms gives this maze-zushi a tantalizing aroma. Fresh shiitake are ideal for this recipe, but if you can't get them, reconstitute 5 dried mushrooms by simmering in enough water to cover for 15 minutes.

Ingredients for 2 servings:

5 fresh shiitake mushrooms (2¾ oz / 80 g total)
2 Tbsp saké
2 tsp soy sauce
3 thin green spring onions
11½ oz (330 g, or 1¾ cups) prepared sushi rice

1   Remove the shiitake stems and cut the caps into thin slices. Chop onions.

2   Combine the mushrooms, saké, and soy sauce in a small pan over medium heat. Cook until mushrooms begin to soften, about 2 minutes.

3   Put the sushi rice in a bowl. Add the shiitake and green spring onions and mix gently until all ingredients are combined. Transfer to a serving dish.

Lotus Root with Balsamic Vinegar Maze-zushi

The balsamic vinegar gives this maze-zushi a sophisticated flair. You can use daikon radish or turnip in place of lotus root, if you wish. This recipe also calls for a lot of shiso, which adds a special aroma.

Ingredients for 2 servings:

10 shiso leaves
⅔ of a small lotus root (3½ oz / 100 g total)
1 Tbsp balsamic vinegar
½ tsp soy sauce
11½ oz (330 g, or 1¾ cups) prepared sushi rice

1   Layer the shiso leaves in stacks of 5, roll up, and chiffonade finely. Slice the lotus root into ¼ in (6 mm) rounds, then cut crosswise to make small pieces.

2   Combine the lotus root, balsamic vinegar, and soy sauce in a covered saucepan over medium heat. When steam begins to come out from under the lid, turn the heat to low and allow to simmer for 3–4 minutes, turning lotus root occasionally. Remove from heat and transfer to a bowl to cool.

3   Combine the sushi rice, lotus root, and shiso in a bowl or wooden sushi tub and toss gently to mix. Transfer to a serving dish.

Okra Mixed with Tofu

The soft, slippery textures of okra and tofu really complement each other in this dish, which is melt-in-your-mouth good. White miso is called for here, but other kinds work equally well. If you use darker miso, reduce the amount, as it will be saltier than white miso.

Ingredients for 2 servings:

6 okra pods (1½ oz / 40 g total)
⅓ block firm tofu (3½ oz / 100 g total)
2 tsp white miso

1   Drain the tofu in a strainer or colander for 5–10 minutes.

2   Bring plenty of water to a boil in a medium saucepan. Blanch the okra pods for 1 minute and drain. When cool enough to handle, slice into ¼ in (8 mm) rings.

3   Combine the tofu and white miso in a bowl, mixing well to distribute the miso evenly. Add the okra and mix again. Transfer to a serving dish.

Roasted Broccoli and Cauliflower Maze-zushi

Make sure the roasted broccoli and cauliflower are completely coated with the vinegar mixture. Then combine thoroughly with the rice to make a very easy sushi dish. The lightly pickled vegetables are also delicious on their own.

Ingredients for 2 servings:

about quarter of a head, or 5 flowerets broccoli (1¾ oz / 50 g total)
about a sixth of a head, or 4 flowerets cauliflower (1¾ oz / 50 g total)
1⅔ Tbsp vinegar
2 tsp sugar
⅓ tsp salt
11½ oz (330 g, or 1¾ cups) warm cooked rice, not seasoned

1   Cut broccoli and cauliflower into bite-sized pieces and place on a stovetop grill over high flame. Roast, turning from time to time, until browned.

2   Combine the vinegar, sugar, and salt in a bowl and stir to dissolve sugar and salt. Add vegetables and mix well.

3   Add cooked rice to the vegetables and mix gently to combine. Transfer to a serving dish.

Cucumber Soup (side dish) recipe is on p. 102

Watercress and Hot Sauce Maze-zushi

The spicy simmered watercress goes surprisingly well with the sushi rice. Sliced red radishes, green peas, or beans also make fine additions. Feel free to increase or decrease the amount of hot sauce to match your taste.

Ingredients for 2 servings:

3 ½ oz (120 g, or 3 cups) watercress, trimmed, washed, and dried
½ sweet red bell pepper (3½ oz / 75 g total)
¼ cup frozen corn
1 tsp hot sauce such as Tabasco
2 Tbsp saké
2 Tbsp water
2 tsp soy sauce
11½ oz (330 g, or 1¾ cups) prepared sushi rice

1   Cut watercress into 2 in (5 cm) lengths. Cut the red bell pepper into ⅜ in (1 cm) squares. Bring plenty of water to a boil, add the corn and blanch for 1 minute, then drain.

2   Combine the watercress, Tabasco sauce, saké, water and soy sauce in a saucepan over medium heat. Bring to a boil, lower heat and simmer for 1 minute, stirring occasionally. Remove from heat and transfer to a bowl to cool.

3   Combine the sushi rice, red bell pepper, corn, and simmered watercress in a bowl. Toss gently to mix. Transfer to a serving dish. Garnish with watercress.

Steamed Mixed Vegetable Chirashi-zushi

Because you can use leftover sushi rice and any vegetables you have on hand, this makes a great last-minute meal. It doesn't matter what you use—anything will taste good.

Ingredients for 2 servings:

10 green beans
¼ carrot (1 oz / 50 g total)
6 fresh shiitake mushrooms (3½ oz / 100 g total)
3 Tbsp shredded pickled ginger
11½ oz (330 g, or 1¾ cups) sushi rice

1   Top and tail the green beans and snap or cut into bite-sized lengths. Cut the carrot in half lengthwise, and then slice each half lengthwise into thin strips. Remove the stem from the shiitake mushrooms and cut into bite-sized pieces.

2   Lay a square of cooking parchment in the steamer basket and spread the sushi rice on top of it. Arrange the vegetables on the rice, and top with pickled ginger. Steam for 6–7 minutes.

3   Carefully transfer all ingredients from the steamer to a serving dish and mix gently together before serving.

Avocado, Radish, Dried Shiitake and Watercress Chirashi-zushi

The vinegar rice is really complemented by the radish and watercress, resulting in a tasty, bittersweet sushi dish. The avocado will change color if left out, so if there's going to be some time before serving, sprinkle with a little lemon juice to prevent browning.

Ingredients for 2 servings:

3 dried shiitake (½ oz / 15 g total)
5 oz (150 ml) water
1½ Tbsp mirin
1½ Tbsp soy sauce
⅔ avocado
1 bunch watercress, washed and trimmed (2 oz / 60 g total)
7 red radishes, washed and trimmed (2½ oz / 70 g total)
11½ oz (330 g, or 1¾ cups) prepared sushi rice

1   One hour ahead of time, put the shiitake and water in a saucepan and allow to soak. After an hour, remove the mushrooms, squeeze out excess liquid, slice thinly and return to pan. Add mirin and soy sauce and place over medium heat. Bring to a boil, then turn heat to low, and simmer for 10 minutes, then remove from heat. Place the shiitake in a small bowl to cool, reserving the cooking liquid in a separate bowl.

2   Bring plenty of water to boil in a medium saucepan. Blanch the watercress for 1 minute, then cool immediately under running water. Cut into 2 in (5 cm) lengths and combine with the shiitake cooking liquid.

3   Cut the avocado into ⅜ in (1 cm) pieces. Slice radishes thinly.

4   Combine the sushi rice with the sliced shiitake, tossing gently to mix well. Divide the rice between 2 serving dishes, and top each serving with watercress, avocado, and radish.

Simple Umeboshi Plum and Vegetable Chirashi-zushi

This is such an easy dish. As long as you have umeboshi plums, you can use just about any vegetables you like. I do recommend that you include mushrooms, for their aroma.

Ingredients for 2 servings:

2 umeboshi plums
3½ oz (100 g) shimeji mushrooms
15 snow peas
1 Tbsp vinegar
½ Tbsp sugar
11½ oz (330 g, or 1¾ cups) leftover cooked rice, not seasoned

1   Remove the pits from the plums and break up the pulp with the back edge of a knife. Remove the hard base of the mushrooms and separate into bite-sized pieces. Remove the strings from the snow peas. Combine the sugar and vinegar and mix until sugar dissolves.

2   Divide the rice into 2 heat-proof bowls and sprinkle half of the sugar and vinegar mixture over each. Put half the umeboshi plum, mushrooms, and snow peas on each bowl of rice.

3   Bring water to boil in a steamer. Place the bowls directly in the steamer, cover, and steam for 5 minutes. Remove the bowls from the steamer and gently mix ingredients together.

Quick-pickled Cucumber Inari-zushi

The quick-pickled cucumber adds a delightful spark to this inari-zushi. It's also a nicely balanced dish, thanks to the protein in the inari pouch and the abundance of vegetables.

Ingredients for 2 inari-zushi:

1 medium Japanese cucumber (3½ oz / 100 g total)
¼ tsp salt
1 Tbsp vinegar
1 Tbsp white sesame seeds
4 oz (110 g, or a generous ½ cup) prepared sushi rice
2 prepared inari pouches (see p. 82)

1   Slice the cucumber into thin rounds and place in a bowl, dust with salt and leave for 1 minute. Massage with hands, and tilt the bowl over the edge of the sink and squeeze of the expelled liquid from the cucumbers. Sprinkle with the vinegar and let stand for 5 minutes.

2   Refer to the directions on p. 82 to fill the inari pouches with the sushi rice. Fold over the edges of the pouches and heap cucumbers on top of the rice. Top with sesame seeds.

Carrot and Koya-dofu Inari-zushi

photograph on facing page

The carrot and freeze-dried tofu together make a fill-ing that has a warm sweetness. If you use a generous amount on top of the rice in the inari pouches, it makes a substantial dish.

Ingredients for 2 inari-zushi:

2 in (5 cm) length carrot (1 oz / 30 g total)
½ square Koya-dofu in Marinade, p. 52
½ Tbsp soy sauce
½ Tbsp mirin
4 oz (110 g, or a generous ½ cup) prepared sushi rice
2 prepared inari pouches (see p. 82)

1   Cut the carrot in half crosswise, then lengthwise into thin sheets. Stack the sheets and cut into fine slivers. Squeeze the water out of the koya-dofu and chop in slivers.

2   Combine the carrot, koya-dofu, soy sauce, and mirin in a small pan over medium heat. Cook for 2 minutes, or until the carrots are just soft.

3   Refer to the directions on p. 82 to fill the inari pouches with the sushi rice. Fold over the edges of the pouches and heap the carrot and koya-dofu mixture on top of the rice.

Deep-fried Lotus Root Chirashi-zushi

It's surprising how different this chirashi-zushi is from the one with simmered lotus root. This dish is crunchy, filling, and delicious.

Ingredients for 2 servings:

⅓ cup frozen green peas
1 Tbsp dried hijiki
½ medium lotus root (2¾ oz / 80 g total)
oil for deep frying
1⅓ Tbsp rice vinegar
¼ tsp salt
11½ oz (330 g, or 1¾ cups) prepared sushi rice

1   Bring a generous amount of water to boil in a medium saucepan. Blanch the peas for 1 minute and remove, reserving the cooking water. Blanch the hijiki for 30 sec-onds. Drain both ingredients well, then mix gently into the sushi rice.

2   Cut lotus root into thin slices. Pour about 2 in (5 cm) of oil in a deep, straight-sided frying pan and heat to 380°F (190°C). Use tongs or cooking chopsticks to place the lotus root slices, uncoated, in the oil. Cook until browned, about 3 minutes, turning once or twice. Transfer to a paper towel-lined rack or plate to drain. Sprinkle with vinegar, and then with salt.

3   Put sushi rice into a serving dish and arrange fried lotus root on top.

Pickled Turnip and Okra Maze-zushi

These pickles keep for a long time in the refrigerator, so double the quantities if you want extra. They're good with rice, but I sometimes even put them between two slices of fresh bread for a tasty sandwich.

Ingredients for 2 servings:

1 small Japanese-style turnip (kabu) (3½ oz / 100 g total)
5 okra pods (1 oz / 35 g total)
3 Tbsp plus 1 tsp vinegar
3 Tbsp plus 1 tsp mirin
⅓ cup plus 2 Tbsp (100 ml) water
½ tsp salt
11½ oz (330 g, or 1¾ cups) warm cooked rice, not seasoned

1   Bring plenty of water to boil in a medium saucepan. Blanch the okra for 1 minute. Trim the turnip and cut into ⅛ in (4 mm) slices. Place vegetables in a sturdy glass or plastic container with a tight-fitting lid.

2   Combine the vinegar, mirin, water, and salt in a small pan over medium heat and bring to a near boil, then remove from heat. Stir to dissolve the salt, allow the liquid to cool somewhat, then pour over turnip and okra. Refrigerate for at least half a day. (Pickles will keep for 5 or 6 days in the refrigerator.)

3   Remove the turnip and okra from the pickling liquid, reserving 2 Tbsp of the liquid. Cut the turnip into bite-sized pieces and chop the okra coarsely.

4   Mix the 2 Tbsp pickling liquid with the warm rice. Add the chopped turnip and okra and toss to mix well. Transfer to a serving dish.

Deep-fried Tororo Yam and Salted Cucumber Maze-zushi

The yam turns a beautiful brown color when fried. Frying them adds another dimension of sweetness, and they go very well with the lightly salted cucumber.

Ingredients for 2 servings:

2½ in (6 cm) length tororo yam (nagaimo) (2½ oz / 70 g total)
oil for frying
⅔ Japanese cucumber (2½ oz / 70 g total)
¼ tsp salt
11½ oz (330 g, or 1¾ cups) prepared sushi rice

1   Cut the yam into ⅜ in (1 cm) cubes. Thinly slice the cucumber and place in a small bowl. Sprinkle with salt and massage by hand for about 1 minute. Tilt the bowl over the edge of the sink and squeeze out the expelled liquid.

2   Pour about 2 in (5 cm) of oil in a deep, straight-sided frying pan and heat to 380°F (190°C). Use a metal slotted spoon or long-handled metal sieve to place the yam cubes, uncoated, into the oil. Cook until browned, about 3 minutes, turning once or twice with cooking chopsticks. Transfer to a paper towel–lined rack or plate to drain.

3   Mix cucumber and fried yam into the sushi rice, tossing gently to combine. Transfer to a serving dish.

More Recipes: Sushi

Balsamic-simmered Celery Nigiri-zushi

photograph on page 2

The green crunchiness of the celery is a fine contrast to the soft, piquant sushi rice. For another dimension of flavor, smear a bit of prepared wasabi on the nigiri pieces before topping them with the celery.

Ingredients for 4 pieces:

½ stalk celery (2 oz / 60 g total)
1 Tbsp balsamic vinegar
1 tsp soy sauce
3 oz (80 g, or a scant ½ cup) prepared sushi rice

1   Cut celery crosswise into 2 in (5 cm) pieces, then slice each piece thinly lengthwise to make short strips.

2   Combine the celery, balsamic vinegar and soy sauce in a covered saucepan over medium-high heat. When steam begins to come out from under the lid, turn the heat to low and let steam for 3 minutes. Remove from heat and transfer to a bowl to cool.

3   Divide the sushi rice and shape into 4 pieces. Divide the celery into 4 portions and arrange the celery strips attractively on each nigiri piece. Place on a serving dish.

Cucumber and Yuzukosho Paste Nigiri-zushi

photograph on page 2

The aroma of the yuzukosho paste adds an ethereal touch. The simmering time for the cucumber can be adjusted to your taste, but I recommend cooking it until it is soft, as this goes best with the rice.

Ingredients for 4 pieces:

½ Japanese cucumber (1¾ oz / 50 g total)
1 Tbsp water
1 Tbsp saké
¼ tsp yuzukosho paste
½ tsp soy sauce
3 oz (80 g, or a scant ½ cup) prepared sushi rice

1   Cut the cucumber crosswise into 2 pieces, then cut each piece lengthwise into 4–6 slices.

2   Combine the cucumber, water, saké, yuzukosho paste, and soy sauce in a saucepan over medium heat. When the liquid boils, turn the heat to low and simmer for 4–5 minutes, or until liquid has evaporated. Remove from heat and transfer to a bowl to cool.

3   Divide the sushi rice and shape into 4 pieces. Arrange 2 or 3 cucumber strips attractively on each nigiri piece. Place on a serving dish.

Dried Shredded Daikon Maze-zushi

photograph on page 2

For the sake of convenience, the amounts given to make the daikon-carrot mixture are greater than needed for the maze-zushi. Enjoy the leftovers as a side dish or salad. The mixture will keep for 4–5 days in the refrigerator.

Ingredients for 2 servings:

⅓ cup dried daikon strips (kiriboshi daikon) (1¾ oz / 50 g total)
1 small carrot (2½ oz / 70 g total)
1½ Tbsp soy sauce
11½ oz (330 g, or 1¾ cups) prepared sushi rice

1   Put the daikon strips in a colander or strainer and rinse under cool running water. Drain and cut into 1¼ in (3 cm) lengths. Cut the carrot into matchsticks or a thick julienne.

2   Put the daikon strips, carrot and soy sauce into a saucepan and add just enough water to cover. Bring to a boil over medium heat. Lower the heat and simmer until almost all the liquid has evaporated. Remove from heat, drain, and allow to cool slightly. Measure out ⅓ cup of the mixture, saving the rest to eat later.

3   Combine the reserved ⅓ cup of the daikon and carrot mixture with the sushi rice, tossing gently to mix. Transfer to a serving dish.

Mixed Mushroom Maze-zushi

photograph on page 2

This is great comfort food—the mushrooms are tender, the rice is moist, and the ginger adds a warming touch.

Ingredients for 2 servings:

1¾ oz (50 g, or ½ package) shimeji mushrooms (use buna-shimeji if available)
3 fresh shiitake mushrooms (1¾ oz / 50 g total)
1 medium king oyster mushroom (1¾ oz / 50 g total)
2 tsp soy sauce
2 Tbsp saké
1 Tbsp minced ginger
11½ oz (330 g, or 1¾ cups) prepared sushi rice

1   Cut away the thick base of the shimeji mushrooms and pull the clusters apart into bite-sized pieces. Discard the hard stems of the shiitake, brush off any dirt from the caps, and slice thinly. Slice the king oyster mushroom thinly.

2   Combine all mushrooms, ginger, soy sauce, and saké in a covered saucepan over medium heat. When steam begins to come out from under the lid, turn the heat to low and simmer uncovered for 3–4 minutes, or until liquid is evaporated. Remove from heat and allow to cool slightly.

3   Combine the simmered mushrooms with the sushi rice in a bowl or wooden sushi tub. Toss gently to mix well. Transfer to a serving dish.

Deep-fried King Oyster Mushroom Nigiri-zushi

photograph on page 10

These mushrooms have a toothsome, chewy texture like abalone. A little salt enhances the flavor, but it's also nice to top the finished nigiri with a few extra drops of olive oil.

Ingredients for 4 pieces:

1 large king oyster mushroom (2¾ oz / 80 g total)
oil for frying
pinch salt
3 oz (80 g, or a scant ½ cup) sushi rice

1   Brush off or gently wash the king oyster mushroom and cut off the hard base of the stem. Cut lengthwise into slices ⅓ in (5 mm) wide.

2   Pour about 2 in (5 cm) of olive oil into a deep, straight-sided cold frying pan and heat to about 365°F (180°C). Use tongs or cooking chopsticks to put the mushroom slices into the hot oil. Fry, turning once or twice, until crisp and brown, about 3 minutes. Transfer to a paper towel–lined rack or plate and allow to drain.

3   Divide the sushi rice and shape into 4 nigiri pieces. Place a slice or two of mushroom on top of each nigiri piece, and sprinkle with salt. Arrange on a serving dish.

Deep-fried Japanese Leek Maki-zushi

photograph on page 10

As simple as this hoso-maki may be, it's unbelievably delicious. Black pepper and sushi rice may sound like an odd coupling, but with the leek it makes a divine combination. This is an excellent dish to serve with a glass of beer or wine.

Ingredients for 1 roll:

1 Japanese leek or young leek, about 6 in (15 cm) long (2 oz / 60 g total)
oil for frying
pinch salt
coarsely ground black pepper, to taste
3 oz (80 g, or a scant ½ cup) sushi rice
½ sheet nori

1   Cut the leek in half lengthwise, then slice each half lengthwise into thin strips.

2   Pour about 2 in (5 cm) of oil in a deep, straight-sided frying pan and heat to 380°F (190°C). Use tongs or cooking chopsticks to place the leek strips, uncoated, into the oil. Cook until browned, about 3 minutes, turning once or twice. Transfer to a paper towel–lined rack or plate to drain. Sprinkle with salt.

3   Assemble and roll the sushi using either a makisu or plastic wrap and a towel as described in the hoso-maki instructions on p. 50. Lay the fried leek on top of the rice and sprinkle with black pepper, to taste, then roll. Cut the roll in half crosswise, then lay the halves side-by-side and cut into thirds, wiping the knife with a damp cloth after each cut. Arrange on a serving dish.

Burdock Root Steamed with Soy Sauce Maki-zushi

photograph on page 11

The burdock root stays crunchy even after steaming, and the flavor of the root is so deep that you really don't need to add any flavoring. Still, I sometimes like to dip this sushi in wasabi and soy sauce.

Ingredients for 1 roll:

8 in (20 cm) length burdock root (2 oz / 60 g total)
1 tsp soy sauce
3 oz (80 g, or a scant ½ cup) prepared sushi rice
½ sheet nori

1   Scrape skin off of burdock root with a knife, and cut in half crosswise. Cut each half in quarters lengthwise.

2   Put the burdock root in a heat-proof bowl and pour soy sauce over, tossing briefly to coat. Bring water to a boil in a steamer and steam the burdock root for 5 minutes.

3   Assemble and roll the sushi using either a makisu or plastic wrap and a towel as described in the hoso-maki instructions on p. 50. Cut the roll in half crosswise, then lay the halves side-by-side and cut into thirds, wiping the knife with a damp cloth after each cut. Arrange on a serving dish.

Japanese Leek Steamed with Miso Nigiri-zushi

photograph on page 11

Steaming makes the leeks juicy, soft, and deliciously sweet. And the flavor of the miso goes like a dream with the sushi rice. It's perfect for serving hot on a chilly day. If they are available, use the long Japanese naganegi instead of leeks.

Ingredients for 4 nigiri pieces:

1 small Japanese leek or young leek (3¾ oz / 100 g total)
½ Tbsp miso (red or white)
3 oz (80 g, or a scant ½ cup) prepared sushi rice

1   Trim the tops and roots from the leek. Slice in half lengthwise, then cut each half into 2 in (5 cm) lengths.

2   Put leeks in a heat-proof bowl. Add miso and massage by hand for about a minute. Bring water to boil in a

steamer and steam the leek-miso mixture for 4–5 minutes or until soft. Remove from steamer and stir to mix.

3   Divide sushi rice and shape into 4 nigiri pieces. Arrange steamed leek on top of each nigiri piece, then place on a serving dish.

Deep-fried Burdock Root Nigiri-zushi

The sweet-and-sour flavor and crunchiness of the burdock root is just wonderful. Sometimes I just like to serve the fried vegetable without rice as a snack, like potato chips.

Ingredients for 4 pieces:

6 in (15 cm) length burdock root (1¾ oz / 50 g total)
oil for frying
½ Tbsp mirin
½ Tbsp vinegar
½ tsp soy sauce
3 oz (80 g, or a scant ½ cup) sushi rice

1   Scrub the burdock root well and peel if desired. Cut in half crosswise, then slice each piece lengthwise into thin strips.

2   Pour about 2 in (5 cm) of oil in a deep, straight-sided frying pan and heat to 380°F (190°C). Use tongs or cooking chopsticks to place the burdock strips, uncoated, in the oil. Cook until browned, about 3 minutes, turning once or twice. Combine mirin, vinegar, and soy sauce in a small bowl. Briefly toss the fried burdock root in the mixture to coat and let sit for 3 minutes.

3   Divide the sushi rice and shape into 4 nigiri pieces. Place fried burdock root on top of each nigiri piece and arrange on a serving dish.

Side Dishes

Spinach with Sesame and Vinegar

photograph on page 59

Sprinkling on the soy sauce and then squeezing it out again heightens the flavor of the spinach and keeps it from getting too watery.

Ingredients for 2 servings:

½ bunch spinach (3½ oz / 100 g total)
1 tsp soy sauce
1 tsp dashi stock (see p. 13) or water
2 Tbsp ground toasted white or black sesame seeds
1 Tbsp vinegar
½ Tbsp soy sauce

1   Bring plenty of water to boil in a large saucepan. Have a large bowl of cold water in the sink. Blanch the spinach in boiling water for about 30 seconds—until it turns bright green—then pull it out with tongs or chopsticks and plunge into cold water to fix the color.

2   Squeeze the water from the spinach, twisting it to form a long roll. Slice the roll into fifths and place in a bowl with the soy sauce and dashi. Mix well, then tilt the bowl over the sink and squeeze out the liquid by hand.

3   Put spinach in a bowl and mix with sesame seeds, vinegar, and ½ Tbsp soy sauce. Transfer to a serving dish.

Spinach Hitashi

photograph on page 68

Adding the soy sauce and dashi stock and then squeezing it out, as described in the second step of this recipe, is the trick to making delicious hitashi. This technique, called "soy sauce washing," makes the difference between a delicious fresh spinach dish and one that is watery and not as tasty.

For 2 servings:

½ bunch spinach (3½ oz / 100 g total), trimmed and washed
1 tsp soy sauce
1 tsp dashi stock (see p. 13) or water
½ tsp soy sauce, or to taste
2 tsp white sesame seeds, or to taste

1   Bring plenty of water to boil in a large saucepan. Have a large bowl of cold water in the sink. Blanch the spinach in boiling water for about 30 seconds—until it turns bright green—then pull it out with tongs or chopsticks and plunge into cold water to fix the color.

2   Squeeze the water from the spinach, twisting it to form a long roll. Slice the roll into fifths and place in a bowl with the soy sauce and dashi. Mix well, then tilt the bowl over the sink and squeeze out the liquid by hand.

3   Arrange the spinach in a serving dish and season to taste with additional soy sauce and sesame seeds.

Cucumber Soup

photograph on page 88

Cold cucumber soup is well known, but this hot soup is also very tasty. If you'd like, add some chopped shiso or grated ginger to add a bit of spice.

Ingredients for 2 servings:

1 Japanese cucumber (3½ oz / 100 g total)
1¼ cups (300 ml) dashi stock (see p. 13)
1 Tbsp saké
¼ tsp salt
1 tsp soy sauce
1 Tbsp white sesame seeds

1   Slice the cucumber into thin rounds.

2   Place the dashi in a saucepan over medium-high heat and bring to a boil. Add cucumber, lower the heat to medium, and cook for 2 minutes more. Add saké, salt, and soy sauce, and remove from heat.

3   Ladle into individual bowls to serve and garnish with white sesame seeds.

Daikon and Wakame Miso Soup

The simple combination of chirashi-zushi and a soup makes quite a complete menu. A clear soup is nice, but this miso soup adds flavor to the menu. Adding strips of abura-age (deep-fried tofu) to the soup makes it even richer.

Ingredients for 2 servings:

1¼ cups (300 ml) dashi stock (see p. 13)
1½ in (3 cm) round of daikon radish (3½ oz / 100 g total)
1 Tbsp dried cut wakame
1 Tbsp miso
1 Tbsp chopped chives or green onion, or to taste

1   Peel the daikon and slice into ⅛ in (4 mm) rounds. Stack the rounds and cut into matchsticks.

2   Combine the dashi and daikon in a saucepan over medium-high heat and bring to a boil. Lower the heat and simmer for 3-4 minutes, until daikon is soft.

3   Add the wakame. Put the miso in a small bowl and add a ladleful of dashi, then blend to dissolve the miso. Add the dissolved miso to the soup and remove from heat. Stir well and serve. Garnish with chopped chives or green onions.

Party Sushi: Temaki-zushi

Temaki-zushi, or hand-roll sushi, is great for parties, where you can put out the fillings and let your guests make their own. Just prepare the sushi rice and fillings in advance. One or more toppings can be used in a single roll. In addition to the cooked toppings below, you can have julienned cucumbers, avocado slices, blanched steamed carrot strips, blanched spinach . . . the list of possible ingredients is as endless as your imagination!

Ingredients to serve 5-6:

sushi rice prepared from 2½ US cups, or 18 oz / 510 g total) of dry rice (see p. 13)
10 or more nori sheets, cut in half
3 or more prepared toppings

1   With dry hands, take a piece of nori and lay it shiny-side-down on your non-dominant hand so that the long side runs in the same direction as your fingertips.

2   Scoop a handful (about 3 Tbsp, or 40g) of sushi rice and lay it on the bottom part of the nori (on your palm). Spread the rice to cover the bottom third of the nori, without going all the way to the edges.

3   Use a wetted finger to make an indentation in the center of the rice, parallel to the short edge of the nori rectangle. Carefully lay one or more kinds of topping in the indentation, being careful not to add too much.

4   Roll up into a cone shape. Take the bottom corner of the nori that is closest to your body (furthest from your thumb) and bring it diagonally up and across the rice and toppings, cupping your palm to get the cone started. Continue rolling to make a tight cone shape.

5   Arrange on a serving platter, with saucers of soy sauce for dipping. Serve as soon as possible, or the nori will get soggy.

SAMPLE FILLINGS

CUCUMBERS WITH WASABI AND SOY SAUCE

1 Japanese cucumber (3½ oz / 100 g total)
½ tsp prepared wasabi, or to taste
1 tsp soy sauce

1   Cut the cucumber into 2 in (5cm) long pieces, then quarter each piece lengthwise.

2   Combine wasabi and soy sauce in a bowl. Add cucumber spears, mix to coat, and let stand for at least 3 minutes.

ROASTED ASPARAGUS COATED IN LEMON MISO

5 stalks asparagus (5¼ oz / 150 g total)
1 Tbsp lemon juice
½ Tbsp miso (any kind)

1   Cut off the hard base of the asparagus spears and peel off any tough skin.

2   Lay the asparagus on a stovetop grill over high heat. Roast, turning periodically, until the asparagus is just tender and the skin begins to blacken. Remove from heat.

3   Mix the lemon and miso in a small bowl until well blended. Add the asparagus and mix to coat.

Tools

While these tools are not absolutely necessary to make the recipes in this book, they are practical and easy to use if you have them around. Some of them can be found in any kitchen goods shop, some in Asian markets, and most are easily found on the internet. If you must prioritize, a kitchen scale, grater, and a sushi rolling mat makes cooking in general a lot easier.

If you are ever visiting Tokyo, I highly recommend a visit to the Kappa-bashi area, where kitchen goods are sold wholesale. It's easy to spend a day oohing and ahing over the incredible array of tools and dishes, even if you're not buying anything.

Oshi-zushi mold (*kata*): Oshi-zushi molds may come in different sizes, but they all have the same basic components. Note the slots on the sides of this one, which serve as a guide for slicing the finished pressed sushi. Always make sure the sushi mold is moist before pressing your sushi.

Sushi rice tub (hangiri): This wooden tub combines a large surface area—which helps dissipate the heat and moisture of the cooked rice—with absorbent wood, which also takes in excess moisture from the cooked rice and added seasonings. Rice mixed in a hangiri stays moist without becoming soggy or lumpy. If you don't have a hangiri, a large wooden bowl of any kind (e.g., a salad bowl) works fairly well.

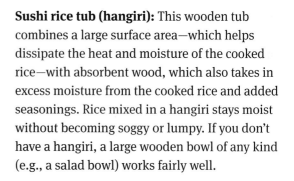

Kitchen scale: Weighing ingredients, especially vegetables, will save a lot of waste and hassle. There's no need for anything fancy—a simple mechanical scale with a plate big enough to hold long or oddly shaped vegetables will meet your needs.

Stovetop grill (*yaki-ami*): This simple tool is used for stovetop grilling of vegetables, but any mesh stovetop grill will work fine.

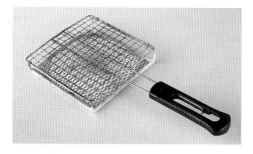

Ceramic grater (*oroshi*): Unlike a typical grater, this tool has no holes; it relies on hard spikes to break up ginger, daikon, or other items into fine pieces.

Rice paddle (*shamoji*): This wide, flat paddle is ideal for incorporating sushi seasoning into rice; it allows you to toss large amounts of rice while causing the least possible damage to the fragile cooked grains.

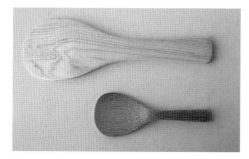

Sushi rolling mats (*makisu*): These flexible mats, made of bamboo woven together with strong thread, are very helpful for making maki-zushi. The large size works for futo-maki (thick rolls), while the thinner mat is used to make hoso-maki (thin rolls). Wash and dry your makisu thoroughly after each use.

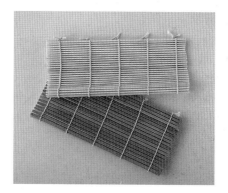

Bamboo steamer: A metal steamer that fits into a covered pot also works for the recipes in this book. A bamboo steamer like the one shown here should sit tightly on top of a deep pot with boiling water. The advantage is that the steam escapes from the bamboo, rather than condensing in the steamer and dripping onto the food.

Cutting Techniques

There are different types of Japanese knives for fish, vegetables, and other ingredients, and while you don't have to worry about matching knives when all your ingredients are vegetables, it's handy to know the various Japanese techniques for wielding your knife on produce. These methods work equally well with either Japanese or Western knives.

Making cubes: Follow the directions for making bars, above. Line up the bars and cut crosswise into ⅜ in (1 cm) cubes.

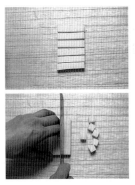

Making matchsticks: Cut the vegetable into 2 in (5 cm) lengths, then cut each length into thin sheets. Finally, cut the sheets lengthwise into thin matchsticks.

Making bars: Cut a 2 in (5 cm) length of the vegetable. Stand on end and slice into ⅜ in (1 cm) slabs. Finally, cut each slab into ⅜ in (1 cm) wide bars.

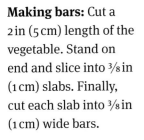

Making fine slivers: Use this technique for Japanese leeks, leeks, or green onions. Cut a length of the vegetable about as long as your middle finger. Score it lengthwise to reach the center of the onion, then spread the layers out so they lie flat on the cutting board. Cut them lengthwise into very fine slivers.

Chopping very finely:
Use this technique for Japanese leeks, leeks, or green onions. Use the upper half of the vegetable (including the green part). Holding the greens, make a lengthwise cut from just below where the leaves separate all the way to the end of the onion. Roll the onion slightly and make another cut. Continue to roll and cut the onion until it is in fine strips held together at the top. Then turn the onion 90 degrees, holding all the strips together, and cut very finely crosswise to make tiny pieces.

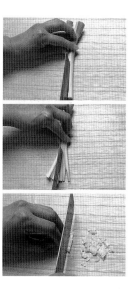

Cutting thin slices:
Bend your fingers holding the vegetable at the first knuckle, where the knife should make the slice, to guide the blade. If your knife is sharp, it should slice cleanly through without any sawing motion. Then move your fingers slightly back to make the next slice.

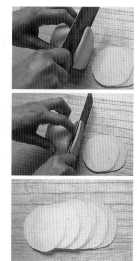

Preparing burdock root (*gobo*): Most Japanese cooks use the back edge of a knife, rather than a peeler, to remove the outer skin from a burdock root. Scrape off all the skin, then rinse under running water. Cut the gobo into slices on a steep diagonal. Stack up the slices and slice them lengthwise into thin matchsticks. Keep in a bowl of vinegar water until you cook them.

Index